HIGHL

44 Vegetarian Restaurants/cafes

Ambica, Leicester	49
Amity Point, Norwich	65
Bobby's, Leicester	49
Butlers, Norwich	66
Chaat House, Leicester	49
Camphill Cafe, Milton Keynes	11
The Cross, Woodbridge	88
Daily Bread Cafe, Cambridge	19
Dedham Centre Tea Room	29
Good Earth, Leicester	49
Greenhouse, Norwich	66
Green House, Mkt Harborough	55
Green House, Tring	44
Hillside vegan cafe, W Runton	61
Holland & Barrett, Bury St Eds	83
Holland & Barrett, Lowestoft	87
Holland & Barrett, Stowmarket	88
Indigo, Leicester	50
Ipswich Food Coop	86
Les Amandines, Diss	63
LevelBest Artcafe, Colchester	28
Mirch Masala x2, Leicester	50
Museum Street Cafe, Ipswich	85
My Kitchen, Leigh-on-Sea	31
Oasis, Attleborough	62
A Pinch of Veg, Ilford	30
Pooja, Wellingborough	77
Pulse, Norwich	66
Rainbow Cafe, Cambridge	17
Red Lion pub, Great Bricett	84
Saffron, Saffron Walden	33
Sardaar, Leicester	50
Sayonara Thali, Leicester	51
Shankar Paubhaji, Leicester	51
Sharmilee, Leicester	51
Shivalli, Leicester	51
Stop the Week, Peterborough	22
Tea House, Norwich	67
Vegeland (vegan), Norwich	67
Veggie World, Milton Keynes	11
Wholefood Planet, Norwich	72
Woody's, Hemel Hempstead	39
World Peace Cafe, Kelmarsh	75

Plus
90 more restaurants & cafes recommended by local veggies and vegans for exceptional menus

Number 15, Norwich	
Old Hall, Beccles	79
Old Red Lion B&B, Castle Acre	60
Rainbow B&B, Bury St Edmunds	80
Swallow Organics, Saxmundham	82
Western House, Cavendish	82
West Lodge, Norwich	58
White House Farm, Woodbridge	81

Other Accommodation

Gables Guesthouse, Bucks	9
Acacia Guesthouse, Cambridge	16
Greenbanks Hotel, Wendling	59
Brick Kilns, Little Plumstead	65

12 Pubs with big veggie menus

Assembly House, Norwich	68
Brick Kilns, Little Plumstead	64
Cambridge Blue, Cambridge	17
Frank's Bar, Norwich	69
Green Man, Fakenham	65
Judes Ferry, Mildenhall	87
King William IV, Heydon	40
New Inn, Wymington	7, 78
Norwich Arts Centre	70
Penny Whistle, Northampton	75
Red Lion, Great Bricett	84
Swan Inn, Hoxne	85

Treats

Farley's Hair Salon, Hitchin	42
Leicester Vegan Fair	55

Animal Sanctuaries

Hillside, Frettenham	61
Hillside, West Runton	61
Redwings, Essex	25
Redwings, Norfolk	62

Plus
79 independent and
80 chain shops for picnic lunches
Local groups to find new friends
Vegetarian caterers

The perfect present for vegetarians, vegans, meat reducers and those who love them (but never knew where to take them)

Collect the set

VEGETARIAN LONDON
160 vegetarian restaurants, cafes and take-aways. 200 more with huge veggie menus. 300 shops. Accommodation. 15 local maps.

"More important than the A-Z."
The Vegetarian Society

VEGETARIAN BRITAIN
Includes in-depth coverage of veggie travel hotspots Bath, Birmingham, Brighton, Bristol, Bournemouth, Cornwall, Devon, Edinburgh, Lake District, Manchester, London, Nottingham, Scottish Highlands, Wales and Yorkshire.
Maps. Indexes for vegan, dog-friendly and children welcome.
Just like this book but 7 times the size!

VEGETARIAN EUROPE
48 destinations in 23 countries including giant Paris section.

"An ideal springboard for that European holiday you always wanted to take, but were unsure about the food."
The Vegetarian Society

www.vegetarianguides.co.uk

Vegetarian Britain 4th edition
part 3:

EAST
of England

Beds, Bucks, Cambs, Essex, Herts,
Leics, Norfolk, Northants, Suffolk

300 places to eat, sleep and shop veggie

Edited by Alex Bourke

Contributors:

Bedfordshire: Alexandra Geen

Buckinghamshire: Mat & Ravi Schencks, Peter Simpson

Cambridgeshire: Dr Cynthia Combe, Roger & Anna Merenyi, Adam Moss

Essex: Jill Adams, Gaynor Armitage, Karin Ridgers

Herts: Adina Farmaner, Lian Brook-Tyler, Dr Cynthia Combe, Rachel & Steve

Leicestershire: Antony Coles, Sue Daniels,
Sophia Howard, Verity Hunt-Sheppard, Ronny Worsey

Norfolk: Derek & Sylvia Land, Tom Loudon at Greenhouse

Northamptonshire: Leafcycles, Mat & Ravi Schencks

Suffolk: Sophie and Stephen Fenwick-Paul, Gemma Sayers

 **Vegetarian Guides**

Vegetarian East of England, 1st edition

by Alex Bourke   ISBN 978-1-902259-12-3
Published October 2009 by Vegetarian Guides Ltd,
PO Box 2284, London W1A 5UH, England
www.vegetarianguides.co.uk   info@vegetarianguides.co.uk
Reprinted with corrections December 2009
Tel 020-3239 8433 (24 hours)   Fax 0870-288 5085   skype veggie_guides
Design and map by Mickaël Charbonnel, Alexandra Boylan & Rudy Penando
Vegetarian Guides logo design: Marion Gillet
Cover photos clockwise: Redwings horses, Indigo chefs Leicester, The Green House Market Harborough, White House Farm B&B, Arjuna Wholefoods, Brick Kilns pub
Printed and bound in Great Britain by QNS, Newcastle upon Tyne

The Small Print:

Restaurants can change their owners or opening hours and sometimes close for holidays. Every effort has been made to ensure the accuracy of information in this book, however it is impossible to account for every detail and mistakes can occur. Before making a special journey, we recommend you call ahead to check details.

© Vegetarian Guides. No part of this book may be reproduced or transmitted in *any* way or by any means, *including the internet*, without the prior written permission of the publisher, other than brief quotations for review purposes. If you post our work on your website surrounded by paid adverts, we will sue you. If you want to review and recommend our books with a link to us, we will happily pay you commission, see www.vegetarianguides.co.uk/affiliate

For free information on the region's attractions, visit East of England Tourist Board:
www.visiteastofengland.com
Tourist information sites for other counties are listed in those chapters.

Vegetarian East: Contents

Veggie Index	i	Ilford	30	**Norfolk**	
Contributors	iii	Leigh-on-Sea	31	Accommodation	58
Area Map	iv	Loughton	32	Animal sanctuaries	61
Contents	1	Manningtree	32	Attleborough	62
Top 10 Days Out	2	Romford	32	Dereham	63
My Favourite Veggie Table	3	Saffron Walden	33	Diss	63
		Southend-on-Sea	33	Fakenham	63
		Upminster	33	Harleston	64
Bedfordshire		Wickford	34	Holt	64
Bedford	5	Wickham Bishops	34	Little Plumstead	64
Dunstable	6	Catering	34	Little Snoring	65
Leighton Buzzard	6	Mail order	35	**NORWICH – hotspot**	**65**
Luton	6	Local groups	35	Sheringham	72
Wymington	7	Chain stores	36	Swaffham	73
				Walsham	73
		Hertfordshire		Wymondham	73
Buckinghamshire		Berkhamstead	38	Chain stores	73
Accommodation	9	Bishops Stortford	38	Local group	73
Amersham	9	Harpenden	38		
Aylesbury	9	Hatfield	39	**Northamptonshire**	
Buckingham	10	Hemel Hempstead	39	Kelmarsh	75
Chesham	10	Hertford	40	Northampton	75
Gerrards Cross	10	Heydon	40	Rushden	77
High Wycombe	11	Hitchin	41	Towcester	77
Marlow	11	Kings Langley	42	Wellingborough	77
Milton Keynes	11	Letchworth	42	Wymington	78
Local group	14	Potters Bar	42	Chain stores	78
Catering	14	Radlett	43		
		Rickmansworth	43	**Suffolk**	
Cambridgeshire		Sawbridgeworth	43	Accommodation	79
Accommodation	16	St. Albans	43	Beccles	82
CAMBRIDGE	**17**	Stevenage	44	Bungay	82
Ely	21	Tring	44	Bury St Edmunds	83
Hauxton	21	Ware	45	Debenham	84
Huntingdon	22	Watford	45	Great Bricett	84
Peterborough	22	Welwyn Garden City	46	Hadleigh	85
Wisbech	22	Chain stores	47	Halesworth	85
Chain stores,	23	Local group	47	Hoxne	85
Local Group	23	Curry delivery	47	Ipswich	85
Catering	23			Lowestoft	87
		Leicestershire		Mildenhall	87
Essex		Ashby de la Zouch	49	Newmarket	87
Animal Sanctuary	25	**LEICESTER – hotspot**	**49**	Southwold	87
Billericay	25	Loughborough	53	Stowmarket	88
Braintree	25	Market Harborough	54	Sudbury	88
Brentwood	26	Chain stores	55	Woodbridge	88
Brightlingsea	26	Local Group	55	Chain stores	89
Chelmsford	26	Leicester Vegan Fair	55	Local Group	89
Clacton-on-Sea	27				
Colchester	28			**A-Z Index**	**90**
Dedham	29			**Locations Index**	**92**
Hockley	30			**Caterers Index**	**92**

Top 10 Veggie Days Out

Welcome to the first vegetarian guide to the East of England. If you're feeling bamboozled by the huge choice of places to visit, stay over and eat out in these nine counties, here to help you get stuck in are my personal **Top 10 Trips**:

1. **NORWICH** makes a fantastic veggie city break. As well as the gorgeous streets around the cathedral, shopping, arts and very friendly locals, there are half a dozen totally unique vegetarian cafes including **Pulse** and **The Greenhouse**, even a vegan Chinese take-away. If you are making a weekend of it, you have a choice of vegetarian B&B's. Many more cafes have heaps of veggie food, while pub fans will love **Frank's Bar** in the centre and the **Brick Kilns** country pub just outside town. (pages 56-8, 60, 67-72)

2. **LEICESTER** is Britain's top destination for veggie curry lovers with a staggering 12 vegetarian restaurants, all but one of them Indian. (pages 48-53)

3 to 8. Beyond the two hotspots, fabulous vegetarian restaurants miles from any other in shopping and sightseeing centres include **Rainbow** in Cambridge (page 17), **My Kitchen** in Leigh on Sea, Southend (31), **Woody's** near Hemel Hempstead (39), **The Green House** in Tring (44), **The Green House** in Market Harborough (55), and **Les Amandines** in Diss (63).

9. **The Red Lion** in Suffolk (page 84) is the region's only 100% vegetarian pub. The county also has six veggie places to stay from camping through to pampering retreats. This guide lists 11 more pubs with amazing veggie food. Stop press: **The Cross** vegetarian restaurant and wine bar has just opened November 2009 in Woodbridge, Suffolk, near White House Farm veggie B&B.

10. Finally for a family day out, **Hillside** and **Redwings** horse and animal sanctuaries are way kinder to animals than zoos and a great reminder of why we became vegetarians in the first place. (pages 25, 61-2)

Whatever your reasons for eating no or less meat, I wish you many magical moments scoffing your way around the region's 40-plus vegetarian cafes and restaurants and 90 more ethnic restaurants that go out of their way to please us, quaffing in country and city pubs with exceptional veggie menus, recharging at delightful bed & breakfasts, and loading up at wholefood depots on treats such as locally made Booja Booja chocolate truffles. Bon appetit et bons voyages!

Alex Bourke
Founder, Vegetarian Guides

Prince and friend at Redwings horse sanctuary (page 62)

My Favourite Veggie Table

Karin Ridgers, Essex
Founder of VeggieVision TV
Author, journalist, PR guru

I love eating at **My Kitchen** in Leigh on Sea – Stuart makes the best soups and vegan cakes. We eat well at home and have no problems bringing our own dairy-free cheese when going out for a pizza.

I'm a vegan because I want the best and kindest diet and the best for the planet. It's my passion to make a difference for animals and make life easier for future vegans.

My son Callum cannot understand why people eat dead animals. He says wonderful things like "Mummy I want to punch them cages" when seeing a zoo on TV.

www.veggievision.tv   –   www.mad-promotions.com   –   www.offthehoof.co.uk

Adrian Ramsay, Norwich
Deputy Leader of the Green Party
Parliamentary candidate for Norwich South

We're very fortunate in Norwich to have a good range of vegetarian food outlets. I love eating at the **Greenhouse** cafe, **Vegeland** Chinese takeaway and **Pulse** restaurant. Plus there are plenty of Indian restaurants with lots of vegan options.

I'm vegan because of my concern at how animals are treated in the meat and dairy industries. One of the reasons I joined the Green Party was to make a difference on animal rights issues.

www.adrianramsay.org.uk

Bedford	5
Dunstable	6
Leighton Buzzard	6
Luton	6
Wymington	7

Bedfordshire

Bedford

Pizza Express, Bedford
Omnivorous pizza restaurant

22 St Peters St, Bedford MK40 2PN (close to the John Bunyan Statue)
Tel: 01234 271124
Open: Mon 11.30-23.00,
Tues-Sat 11.30-24.00, Sun 11.30-23.30
www.pizzaexpress.com for menus and ingredients lists with vegan suitability

This is the description referred to for other branches of this national chain throughout the East of England.

Pizza Express is open long hours and is a handy standby in areas like Bedfordshire without veggie restaurants. Pizzas have vegan bases and can be made without cheese for vegans. In some branches you can bring your own vegan cheese. Vegan starters £2.05 include roasted tomatoes with herbs and olive oil; nuts and seeds roasted with chilli, salt and rosemary; marinated olives. Pizzas and the new leggera (light) pizza (with a hole in the middle filled with salad) £5.90-8.40. Loads of desserts but alas not a single one is vegan, not even the sorbet, and the tiramisu is not vegetarian.

Wine from £3.65 glass, £12.95 bottle. Italian beers £3.30 (330ml bottle). Low alcohol lager £2.55. Spirits from £2.25. Soft drinks £1.55-2.45.

Children welcome and they have their own menu which is almost all veggie but not vegan.

Vegetarian but not vegan items marked on menu, so consult the very detailed ingredient/allergy list or their website if you have a problem with nuts, garlic, tomatoes etc. Vegans beware that some items that are normally vegan in any other Italian restaurant are not here such as bruschetta. However the chain as a whole are more aware of vegan needs than most restaurants and we hope with further encouragement they could become the first national pizza chain to start stocking vegan cheese and offer vegan ice-cream and reap a tidy increase in customers.

Pumpernickel
Health food shop

7 The Arcade, Bedford, MK40 1NS
Tel: 01234-348179
Open: Mon-Fri 9.30-17.30, Sat 9.00-18.00, Sun closed
www.pumpernickel-online.co.uk

Fridge and two freezers with pies, lots of dairy-free foods such as cheeses, tofu, hummus, meat substitutes, pasties, Swedish Glace, Booja Booja. Raw superfoods such as macca, cacao, spirulina, morinda.

Lots of bodycare includes Aubrey, Faith In Nature, Weleda, Jason, Natracare, baby things.

Supplements by Viridian, Solgar, Lifeplan, Nature's Plus, Biocare, lots of sports nutrition. Homeopathy, full range of aromatherapy. Allergy testing once a month. Therapy room.

Clearning products by BioD and Ecover and some refills. Books and magazines.

Whole Foods Bedford
Wholefood shop

1 Thurlow Street, Bus Station Square
Bedford MK40 1LR
Tel: 01234-219618
Open: Mon-Sat 9.00-17.15, Sun closed

Redwood cheese and meat substitutes, Sheese and Scheese, Swedish Glace ice-cream and other brands if you order. Bodycare including Avalon, Faith In Nature, Dead Sea Magik. Women's personal care. Baby bodycare. Ecover refills. Homeopathy. Aromatherapy. Supplements include Nature's Aid, Lifeplan, Vogel.

Bedford

Holland & Barrett
Health food shop

10 Horne Lane, Harpur Centre, Bedford MK40 1TP . Tel: 01234-352 866
Open: Mon-Sat 9.00-17.30, Sun 10-16.00

This branch has a fridge and freezer.

Green Cuisine
Vegetarian & vegan catering

10 Ribble Way, Bedford MK41 7TY
Tel: 01234-347044
tanna.tanna@ntlworld.com

Any function from dinner parties and house parties to wedding receptions for up to 50 people. A typical buffet would include salads, snacks, samosas, bhajias and desserts.

Dunstable

Wok n Buffet
Omnivorous Chinese restaurant

1 Tring Road, Dunstable LU6 2PX
Tel: 01582-661 485
Open: Mon-Sun 12.00-14.30, 18.00-22.30
www.chinesecateringservice.co.uk

Separate vegetarian and vegan menu. Several vegetable mock meat dishes £4.20-7.50 eat-in, £3.20-£7 take-away. Banana fritters £3.50. Desserts from £2.50. House wine £8.50 bottle, £2.80 glass. Children welcome, high chairs. Visa, MC. Previously called Golden Dragon.

Holland & Barrett
Health food shop

Unit 37 Broadwalk North, The Quadrant Centre, Dunstable LU5 4RH
Tel: 01582-609181
Open: Mon-Sat 9.00-17.30, Sun & bank holiday closed

Fridge and freezer.

Leighton Buzzard

Nature's Harvest
Vegetarian wholefood shop

19 North Street, Leighton Buzzard LU7 1EF
Tel: 01525-371 378
Open: Mon-Sat 9.00-17.00, Sun closed

Good for organic and vegan. Fridge has Redwood cheese and meat substitutes, vegan yogurt and date slices. Big freezer with veggie sausages, bacon, burgers, all the Fry's range, vegan ice-cream. Skincare products. Books. Therapy room with homeopathy, massage, reflexology, allergy testing, nutritional advice.

Luton

Pizza Express, Luton
Omnivorous pizza restaurant

The Lodge, 3 Church Street, Luton LU1 3JE
Tel: 01582-456 229
Open: Mon-Sun 11.30-23.00
www.pizzaexpress.com

In a converted Masonic Lodge. Large separate bar for pre-dinner drink. Outisde dining. Baby changing facilities. For menu see Bedford.

Polska Chata
Omni Lebanese-Polish restaurant

14 Wellington Street, Luton LU2 7BQ (in the centre near Town Hall)
Tel: 01582-411412
Open: Sun-Thu 12-22.00, Fri-Sat 12-24.00
www.polskachataluton.co.uk

Formerly the Morrocan/Lebanese restaurant Marrakesh Gate, and while the new Polish menu is 90% meat, the Lebanese menu has the usual starters from £2, or have mixed mezze for 2 £6.50. Lunch mains £4, evening £5, such as fried aubergine, tomato, onions and chickpeas with rice; or veg stir-fry. Lunch falafel and chips with soft drink £3.50. Wine £2.50 glass, £3.50 large glass, £9.95 bottle. Beer £2.50. Juice cocktail £2. Children welcome, high chairs. Visa, MC.

First Health
Health food shop

87-88 The Market Hall, Arndale Centre, Luton LU1 2TB. Tel: 01582-451170
Open: Mon-Sat 9.00-17.30, Sun closed

Family business, very friendly. Lots of nutrition stuff, dairy-free, gluten-free and intolerances. Fridge and freezer with Redwood, Fry's. The owner does nutritional consultations. Books.

Fair Deal World Shop
Fairtrade shop

605 Hitchin Road, Luton LU2 7UW (Stopsley shopping area). Tel: 01582-416167
Open: Mon-Sat 10.00-18.00, Sun closed
www.fairdealworldshop.com

Fairly traded, cruelty-free and environmenal foods, drinks, household items. Chocolate by Plamil and Organica. Lots of Faith In Nature bodycare. Gifts, toys and puzzles, world music, cards, jewellery, clothes, incense and candles. Ecover and Suma Ecoleaf cleaning products and refills for both. Speakers for groups and schools. Free parking nearby. MC, Visa.

Holland & Barrett
Health food shop

158 Arndale Centre, Luton LU1 2TJ
Tel: 01582-482 574
Open: Mon-Sat 9.00-17.30, Sun 11-17.00

Good sized branch with fridge and freezer.

Wymington

The New Inn
Omnivorous pub-restaurant

Rushden Road, Wymington, Beds NN10 9LN (on the outskirts of Rushden about a mile from the A6, 8 miles north of Bedford.)
Tel: 01933-317618
Pub open: 7 days 12.00-24.00
Food Wed-Sat 12.00-14.0, 18.00-21.00;
Sun lunch 12.00-15.00, no food Tue

Stone-built 300 year old pub that was originally a farm, on the Northants/Beds border. Regulars include a big vegetarian family and children. Several veggie mains all under £7, cooked to order apart from the Glamorgan sausages so they can make it vegan or whatever you want. Burgers with veggie bacon, toad in the hole, pasta dishes. Sunday lunch has a vegetarian roast.
Real ales and ciders. House wine £8 bottle, £3 small glass (175ml), £4 large glass (250ml - buy 2 and get the rest of the bottle free).
Children welcome, big garden and playground, they have rabbits, guinea-pigs and chickens. Outside tables. Dogs welcome in the bar but not the restaurant. Games room with skittles, darts, pool.

Accommodation	9
Amersham	9
Aylesbury	9
Buckingham	10
Chesham	10
Gerrards Cross	10
High Wycombe	10
Marlow	11
Milton Keynes	11
Local group	14
Catering	14

Buckinghamshire

Accommodation
The Gables Guesthouse
Omnivorous bed & breakfast

Brookside, Lillingstone Lovell MK18 5BD (11 miles west of Milton Keynes on the Northants border) Tel: 01280-860680 Train Milton Keynes 11 miles, then taxi www.thegablesbandb.co.uk

One of the owners is veggie and the other runs Greenfeast vegetarian catering company. 2 doubles (one ground floor disabled-friendly with own shower/toilet), 1 twin, £25 per person, £30 single. Children welcome but no special facilities. Dogs by arrangement. Packed lunch £7. 3-course evening meal £15. Organic where possible. TV in rooms, wifi. No-smoking. Cash or cheque with card, no credit cards. Several National Trust properties nearby, Silverstone, the historic market towns of Buckingham and Towcester and also within easy reach of Oxford.

Amersham
Holland & Barrett
Health food shop

43 Sycamore Road, Amersham HP6 5EQ
Tel: 01494-723421
Open: Mon-Sat 08.00-17.30, Sun 10-16.00

Aylesbury
Carlos
Omni Portuguese restaurant & bar

11 Temple Street, off Friar's Square Shopping Complex, Aylesbury HP20 2RN.
Tel: 01296-421 228
Open: every day 08.00-22.00 (last orders), stays open till 01.00, Sun08.00-03.00

14 items on a separate veggie and vegan menu such as nut roast £9.20, chilli beans £9.45, and vegan-fried vegetables in champagne sauce £9.80, all come with veg and side orders of rice, jalapeno chillies etc. Daily veggie special £4.50 such as butternut squash and veg pie with accompaniments. House wine £2.40 glass, bottle £12.25. Children welcome, high chairs. MC, Visa.

Eat As Much As You Like
Omni Chinese buffet restaurant

35-37 New Street, Aylesbury, HP20 2NL
Tel: 01296-422 191
Open: Mon-Sat 12-14.30, 18.00-23.15, Sun 12.00-20.15

Up-market buffet restaurant. Lunchtime £5.95 adult, under-11 £3.95; evening £10.50, children £5.95. 30% suitable for veggies. Licensed. Round the back of Sainsbury's.

Noodle Nation, Aylesbury
Omnivorous Chinese noodle bar

1-3 Bourbon St, Aylesbury HP20 2PZ
Tel: 01296-487773
Open: Mon-Wed 11.30-20.00, Thu-Sat 11.30-23.00, Sun 12.00-21.00
www.noodlebar.net menus

On the outside of Friars Square Shopping building, a popular venue for young and mobile people. Choose a type of rice or noodle such as udon Japanese wheat flour, flat Chinese rice flour, or extra veg instead of noodles, either wok fried or as a big bowl of soup (like Wagamama), then choose your stir-fry such as mixed veg and cashew, or veg with tofu puff and cashew with black bean or Chinese curry or yellow-bean £4.95-5.50. Chunky chips and curry sauce £2.50. Tempura veg with sweet chilli dip £2.60. Dips, extra rice, noddles or veg £1-3.10.

EAST Buckinghamshire

Soft drinks £1.20-1.90. Squeezed juice £2. Wine £3 glass, £12 bottle. Cider and Chinese beer £2.90. Kids menu. Optional 10% service charge. 30p charge for cards under £10. Not suitable for people with severe allergies. 10% student discount. Previously called Noodlebar.

Holland & Barrett
Health food shop

40 Friars Square, Aylesbury HP20 2SP
Tel: 01296-486326. Open: 9.00-17.30, Sat 9.00-18.00, Sun 10.30-16.30

Buckingham
Back to Nature
Health food shop

14 The Cornwalls Centre, off the High Street
Buckingham. MK18 1SB
Tel: 01280-812 694
Open: Mon-Sat 9.15-17.30 (17.00 Thu, Sat)
www.backtonaturebuckingham.com

Chilled and frozen with vegan cheeses and meat subsitutes, soya yogurt, Swedish Glace non-dairy ice-cream. Lots of bodycare including Jason, Weleda, Lavera, Avalon, Dead Sea Magik, Tisserand, Faith In Nature, Dr Bronners. Earth Friendly, Baby bodycare. Women's personal care. BioD and Almawin cleaning producfs. Homeopathy, Tisserand aromatherapy. Health, diet and a few spiritual books. On certain days there is a homeopath, nutritionist, herbalist, relexologist and dowser.

Chesham
Health Right
Health food shop

27 High Street, Chesham HP5 1BG
Tel: 01494-771 267
Open: Mon-Sat 9-17.30, Sun closed
www.healthright.co.uk

Take-away Clive's pies and pasties. They sell soya yoghurt, cheeses and margarines, Swedish glace, Tofutti and carob ices. Baby foods. Supplements and body-building. Bodycare. Aromatherapy, herbal and homeopathy, flower remedies. Water filters. Ecover refills. Books, relaxation CD's. Food intolerance testing. Visa, MC.

Gerrards Cross
Holland & Barrett
Health food shop

2D Station Road, Gerrards Cross SL9 8EL
Tel: 01753-889040
Open: Mon-Sat 9.00-17.30, Sun closed

High Wycombe
Noodle Nation, Hi Wycombe
Omnivorous Chinese noodle bar

5 Crown Lane, High Wycombe HP11 2HF
Tel: 01494-447555
Open: Mon-Wed 11.30-22.00,
Thu-Sat 11.30-23.00, Sun 12.00-21.00
www.noodlebar.net menus

See Aylesbury for menu (above).

Wagamama, High Wycombe

Omnivorous Japanese restaurant

11 Denmark St, Eden, High Wycombe (in the shopping centre near Swan Theatre) HP11 2DB. Tel: 01494-511 302
Open: Sun-Thu 12.00-22.00,
Fir-Sat 12.00-23.00. www.wagamama.com

For menu see Manchester (North). Ground floor, disabled toilet.

Holland & Barrett

Health food shop

6 The Arcade, Octogan Precinct, High Wycombe HP11 2HR
Tel: 01494-526605
Open: Mon-Sat 9.30-18.00, Sun 11-17.00

Marlow

Healthy Stuff

Health food shop

11 Liston Court, Marlow SL7 1ER
Shop: 01628-473684
Health centre: 01628-473687
Open: Mon-Sat 9.30-17.30, Sun closed
http://healthystuff.bttradespace.com

Mostly organic. Fridge with Provamel desserts, and freezer with Clive's Pies and Get Real pies, Goodlife, Swedish Glace, Tofutti and Booja Booja. Supplements include Viridian, Biocare, Higher Nature, A Vogel, Solgar. Baby healthcare. Books. Visa, MC.

Health centre upstairs with acupuncture, allergy testing, Bowen technique, counselling, emotional freedom technique, fertility treatments, flower remedies, homeopathy, hypnotherapy, Swedish, Indian head and maternity massage, McTimoney chiropractic, NLP, nutrition, osteopathy, reflexology, Reiki, women's health.

Milton Keynes - vegetarian

Camphill Cafe

Vegetarian cafe

Camphill Trust, Japonica Lane, off Brickhill Street (V10), Willen Park South, Milton Keynes MK15 9JY. Tel: 01908-235000
Open: Mon-Fri 10.30-16.00, Sat-Sun closed
www.camphill.org.uk/~miltonkeynes

An organisation looking after the interests of people with learning difficulties. Daily hot main course £4.50, sometimes vegan, sandwiches, jacket potatoes, things on toast, afternoon tea. Some of the produce served is grown in the Trust's allotments and organically.

Veggie World

Vegan Chinese restaurant

150-152 Queensway, Bletchley MK2 2RS
Tel: 01908-632 288
Open: Wed-Sat 11.30-14.30,17-22.00
Sun-Tue closed
www.veggie-world.com

100 vegan dishes in the evening and low price set lunches around £3.80, or go a la. carte Lots of meat substitutes like fake chicken and pork, plus tofu, stir-fried veg etc. Starters and soups around £240-2.70. Main courses £5;20-5.50, take-away £3.80. Special rice from £4 eat in. No alcohol, although bring your own wine. Big range of frozen and dried meat substitutes may be purchased for home cooking, so you can buy what you've just had in the restaurant to cook at home, or order online.
Freshly crushed fruit smoothies £2.50-2.80. Tea and coffee £1.40-1.60.
Children welcome, high chair but best to bring your own for very small children.

EAST Buckinghamshire

Milton Keynes – omnivorous
Absolutely Souper
Omnivorous cafe/takeaway

5 Midsummer Place, Milton Keynes MK9 3GB
Tel: 01908-694294
Open: Mon-Sun 10.00-18.00
www.midsummerplace.co.uk

Half the menu is vegetarian with vegan options though many are with cheese so we list the ones that are not. Jacket potato with baked beans, mushrooms or veg chili or Med roast veg, £2.95 one filling, £3.45 two. Vegetarian and vegan soups such as tomato and basil, lentil and herb, £3.45 regular, £3.95 large. Stoops are thicker more filling soups with more bits such as minstrone £3.75 regular, £4.25 large. Bagels are mostly cheese except for Mediterranean veg £2.95.
Frozen fruit smoothies £2.50. Cappuccino, latte, hot choc, coffee all £1.85, large £2.10. Teas £1.20, big £1.35. Everything can also be take-away. No high chairs but kids can have smoothies or ice-lollies. MC, Visa.

Bella Italia, Milton Keynes
Omnivorous Italian restaurant

12 Savoy Crescent, Lower Twelfth St
Milton Keynes MK9 3PU
Tel: 01908-395369
Open: Sun-Thu 10-23.00, Fri-Sat 10-24.00
www.bellaitalia.co.uk

Soup of the day with ciabatta £3.75. Bruschetta £4.25. Mixed side salad £3.25. Spaghetti Napoli £5.95. Giardiniera pizza with several toppings £7.95, extra toppings £1. House wine £12.25 bottle, £3.35-4.35 glass. Beer and cider £2.85-3.45. Children welcome. Outside seating. Large print and braille menus. Accessbile toilets.

Cafe Ganges
Omnivorous Indian restaurant

47 Aylesbury Street, Fenny Stratford, Bletchley, Milton Keynes MK2 2BQ
Tel: 01908-376 332 or 333
Open: Mon-Fri: 17.30-23.00, Fri: 23.30; Sat: 12-14.00 & 17.30-23.30,;Sun: 13-23.00
www.cafegangesfenny.com

Milton Keynes has lots of Indian restaurants. This one does a better than average curry with good veggie thalis. Thali £12.95. Onion bhajis £2.25, samosas £2.75. Biryani, or balti (mild, medium or hot) with nan or rice, £5.95. Vegetarian chilli or green masala, jalfraizy, Bangladeshi bakara, razella, karahi, methi, korma, dopiaza £5.50. Rogan josh, patia, dansak, bhuna, hot madras, very hot vindaloo £4.95. Side dishes £2.50, rice £1.50-2.25, chips 95p.
There is a Sunday buffet but it's almost all non-vegetarian, so go a la carte or try Ganges night Wednesday 5 courses £9.95. Wine from £2.75 glass, £10.45 bottle. Tea or coffee £1.50, with spirits £3.95. Children welcome, no high chair but you can bring one.

Giraffe
Omnivorous International restaurant

39-41 Silbury Arcade Centre, Milton Keynes MK9 3AG. Tel: 01908-392100 (between Waterstones and Marks & Spencer)
Open: Mon-Wed 9.30-21.00, Thu 9.30-22.00, Fri-Sat 9.00-22.00, Sun 9.00-21.00
www.giraffe.net

New chain of restaurants that are lively and very child-friendly. No GM food. Cooked breakfast till midday £5.95, porridge or muesli topped with fruits £4.10. House salad £4.25, hummus with pine nuts and warm naan £4.75, wok-fried edamame soya beans with ginger £4.10. Mezze plate £6.95

(hummus, tabouleh. Indonesian style udon noodle stir-fry £6.95 with shiitake mushrooms, peppers, bok-choy and shallots in coconut and peanut sauce. Burrito or enchilada main £8.25-9.95. Falafel deluxe burger £8.25. No vegan desserts but they could take a fruit bowl off the breakfast menu.

Veggie kids falafel burger & fries £3.95, pasta with tomato sauce or beans on toast £2.95, extra veg 75p-£1. Drinks and fresh smoothies £1.45-2.10.

Smoothies £3.45. Chegworth Valley organic juices £2.85. (Soya) cappuccino £2-£2.40, espresso £1.50, teas and soft drinks £1.75. Beers and cider £2.95-3.50. Wines from £2.65-3.70 glass, £13.25 bottle. Cocktails £5-6.25, non-alcoholic £3.50.

Jaipur

Omnivorous Indian restaurant

599 Grafton Gate East, Milton Keynes, MK9 1AT (corner Avebury Blvd, near station)
Tel: 01908-669796
Open: every day 12.00-23.00
www.jaipur.co.uk

Upmarket and big. Sunday family buffet 12-4pm £12, under-9 half price, has vegetarian dishes. A la carte minimum spend £16. Starters £5, main course curries £7.50, rice £2-3. Separate take-away sectionm 10% cheaper, no delivery. House wine £12.50 bottle, £3.50 glass. No high chairs. No tracksuits, trainers, shorts or vests. MC, Visa.

La Hind

Omnivorous Indian restaurant

Elder House, 502 Elder Gate, Station Square, Milton Keynes MK9 1LR (right by the station)
Tel: 01908-675948
Open: every day 12.00-14.30, 17.30-23.30
Fri lunch closed, Sun 12.00-23.00

Cheaper than Jaipur. Sunday buffet £10.90 till 4pm. Veggie main courses £6.95-7.50, naan £2.30, plain rice £2.30, pilau £2.50. Take-away order 2 mains, get 3rd one free. Rajasthani style. House wine £11.50 bottle, £3.25. Children welcome, 2 high chairs and 4 small seats. MC, Visa.

Red Hot World, Milton Keynes
Omnivorous buffet restaurant & bar

8 Savoy Crescent, Theatre District, Milton Keynes, MK9 3PU
Tel: 01908-609606
Open: every day 12-3.30 17.30-22.30
www.redhot-worldbuffet.com

Gigantic restaurant seating 350 with eat as much as you like buffet with many vegetarian options. Lunch £7.95, Sunday £9.95; evening £12.95, Fri-Sat £14.95. Under-10 half price. Chinese, Italian, Mexican, Indian, Cajun, Japanese and Thai dishes. Spring rolls, samosas, bhajias, pakoras, chips and salsa, potato wedges, spicy veg mix with tortillas, nachos with salad bar; five kinds of made to order pasta with various sauces; noodle bar with udon, rice noodles, tofu and Chinese vegetables; mde to order stir-fry; veg jalfrezi; Mexican exotic veg with roasted pepper sauce. Stacks of desserts including various fruits and liqueurs.

Wine from £11.95 bottle, £3.25 glass. Cocktails £4.45, pitcher £13.95, mocktails £2.75, champagne cocktails £5.95. Spirits £2.25-2.50. Soft drinks £2.95. Coffees all £1.95.

Milton Keynes - omnivorous

Taipan

Omnivorous Oriental restaurant

5 Savoy Crescent, Milton Keynes, MK9 3PU (Avebury Boulevard, by the Theatre)
Tel: 01908-331883
Open: every day 12.00-15.30, 17.30-23.00
www.taipan-mk.co.uk/vegetable.htm

8 vegetarian appetisers £2.30-£4 such as stuffed beancurd roll. 16 main dishes £5.50-8.80, based around aubergine, bean curd, mushrooms and veg. Boiled rice £2. House wine £12 bottle, £3.50 glass. Children welcome, high chairs. MC, Visa.

Wagamama, Milton Keynes

Omnivorous Japanese restaurant

Centre Mk, 7 Sunset Walk, Milton Keynes MK9 3PD. Tel: 01908 238 341
Open: Mon-Sat 12.00-23.00, Sun 12-22.00.
www.wagamama.com

For menu see Manchester (North). Ground floor, disabled toilet.

Milton Keynes - local group

Milton Keynes Vegetarians & Vegans

Peter Simpson, mkvegan475@talktalk.net
Tel: 01908-503 919, 07967 589663
www.mkvegar.makessense.co.uk

Monthly meals at Veggie World restaurant on Wednesdays. Stalls at local events. The website lists additional places to eat in the area.
Peter is the General Secretary of the Vegetarian Cycling & Athletic Club and represents the athletics side. See www.vcac.vegfolk.co.uk

Milton Keynes - shops

Alternatives

Vegetarian health food shop and complementary health centre

Burchard Crescent, Shenley Church End
Milton Keynes MK5 6LP. Tel: 01908-526 524
Open: Mon-Fri 10-18.00, Sat 10-16.00
www.onestopalternatives.co.uk

Chiller cabinet with dairy-free food, fake fish fingers, and drinks. Supplements, skincare, aromatherapy and homeopathy. Baby food and nappies. Books. Services include acupuncture, aromatherapy, beauty therapy, chiropractic, counselling, herbal medicine, homeopathy, hypnotherapy, kinesiology, nutrition, osteopathy, private GP, psychotherapy, reflexology, shiatsu, Swedish and Thai massage. Visa, MC.

Holland & Barrett

Health food shop

Unit 16, The Concourse, the Brunel Centre, Bletchley MK2 2DL. Tel: 01908-642 437
Open: Mon-Sat 9.00-17.30, Sun closed

13 Crown Walk, The Centre, Milton Keynes MK9 3AH. Tel: 01908-607909
Open: Mon-Sat 9.30-18.00, Sun 11-17.00

Quite a big shop with fridge and freezer.

Milton Keynes - catering

Greenfeast

Vegetarian catering

The Gables, 3-4 Brookside, Lillingstone Lovell, Bucks MK18 5BD. Tel: 01280-860680
www.greenfeast.co.uk

Vegetarian and vegan catering in North Bucks and beyond Business meetings, conferences, parties, weddings, christenings, barn dances etc.

Tourist information:
www.visitbuckinghamshire.org

Cambridge is full of students in the winter, and tourists in the summer, who enjoy punting down the river, or chilling in one of the city's many open spaces. The city has a lot of elegance, character and history, a great shopping centre and some excellent health food shops. On Sundays mornings look out for Simon's organic veg stall in the market square, but get there before 12 in case they sell out.

There is only one good vegetarian place, the **Rainbow**, which is recommended by local vegans. A number of other places cater for us, and these are usually packed as demand is high.

Visitor information:
www.visitcambridge.org

16	Accommodation
17	Cambridge
21	Ely
21	Hauxton
22	Huntingdon
22	Peterborough
22	Wisbech
23	Chain stores
23	Local group
23	Catering

Cambridgeshire

Acacia Guesthouse

Detached guest house on the south side of the city offering modern, spacious, well laid out accommodation. There are nine rooms: one single ensuite at £40 per night, one double and one twin at £55 per room per night, two double ensuites and one twin ensuite at £60 per room per night and three family rooms at £70-£85 per room per night (for 3-4 people).

For breakfast choose from a selection of cereals with juice, toast and preserves. A cooked veggie breakfast is available and vegan options can be arranged by request for example, mushrooms on toast. Soya milk and soya spread are also provided on request.

There is no shortage of trendy cafes and restaurants in this university town, most offering veggie food. For a cheaper alternative you could take a picnic to enjoy by the river. Make sure you try punting down the river, but try not to fall in! There are wholefood stores and ethnic grocers in town or if arriving late the Sainsbury's in Coldham's Lane (1.5 miles) or the central one in Sidney Street have a deli and veggie food and are open till 10pm, while Waitrose in Hauxton Road, Trumpington, has a good deli and opens till 9pm (Sat 8pm).

The Botanical Gardens are nearby, and it's only 2 miles by bus to the centre of town. Cambridgeshire has lots of tourist attractions including National Trust sites Anglesey Abbey, Houghton Mill, Wicken Fen and Wimpole Hall as well as English Heritage sites Audley End, Bury St Edmunds Abbey and Denny Abbey. There's also the American Military Cemetry, Ely Cathedral, the Iron Age Fort on Gog Magog Hills, Mountfitchet Castle, Norman Village and an RSPB Nature Reserve all nearby.

Formerly called Dykelands Guest House.

Cambridge

Omnivorous Guest House

157 Mowbray Road
Cambridge
Cambridgeshire CB1 7SP
(south-east of the centre)

Tel: 01223-244 300

Fax: 01223-576798

www.acacia-guesthouse.co.uk

Email: dykelands@ntlworld.com

Train Station: Cambridge 1 mile, then taxi or bus.

Open: all year

Directions: From A10/M11 junction 11 A1309. At seventh set of traffic lights turn right into Long Road. At next roundabout first exit is Mowbray Road.

Parking: available

Children welcome. Cot.

Dogs welcome (in ground floor rooms only)

Visa, MC +3.5%

No smoking throughout

Rooms have tea and coffee making faciltes, televisions and radios.

Cambridge veggie restaurants

Rainbow Cafe

Vegetarian international restaurant

9A Kings Parade, Cambridge CB2 1SJ (opposite Kings College gates)
Tel: 01223-321551
Open: Tues-Sat 10-22.00 (last orders 21.30), Sun-Mon 10.00-16.00
www.rainbowcafe.co.uk

Cambridge's only vegetarian restaurant, and a great place to chill out as a cafe in the afternoon too. Start with soup £3.25, brunch bowl £3.95, garlic bread £2.95 or garden salad £2.95.
Stacks of main courses £7.95-9.95 include 3-bean chili, tacos, pasta, risotto, Ethiopian Mesir-Wat (lentil bowl), Caribbean curry, artichoke parcel, gado gado Indonesian veg, daily specials.
U-10's choices £3.25-3.95 such as pasta or main menu half portions.
Cakes £4.25 include vegan fruit cake. Ice cream is vegan Swedish Glace in 3 flavours. More desserts on the specials board such as vegan crumble.
Wine, beer and cider is vegan organic. Wine £13.95 bottle, £3.45 glass. Beer and cider £3.95. Fairtrade tea and coffees £1.65-1.95.
Vegan, gluten and nut free options clearly indicated. Visa, MC. Vegetarian Society award for best vegetarian cafe.

Cambridge omni restaurants

Al Casbah

Omnivorous Algerian/Med restaurant

62 Mill Road, Cambridge CB1 2AS
Tel: 01223-579500
Open: Mon-Sat 12.00-15.00, Mon-Sun 17.30-23.30
www.al-casbah.com

Mediterranean veggie food galore though they do cook meat in full view. Starters around £3.50 include tabbouleh, hummous, dolma, felafel, Checkchouka mixed peppers with baked aubergine, or a mix for £4.95. Six mains £7.95 are like bigger versions of the starters. House wine £12 bottle, £2.95 glass. Soft drinks £1.50. Coffee or mint tea £1.75. Children welcome, high chairs. Cash or cheque only.

Anatolia

Omnivorous Turkish restaurant

30 Bridge Street, Cambridge CB2 1UJ
Tel: 01223-362372 / 312412
Open: Mon-Sun 12.00-24.00
www.anatolia-cuisine.co.uk

Lots of Turkish veggie mezze dishes £3.55-3.95 or have a mix for £5.65. Mains £10.90 are like big starters. Set lunch till 14.30 £11.95 with starter, main and dessert, pistachio halva appears to be vegan. Wine from £13.50 bottle. Turkish beer £2.95. Coffee £1.95. Soft drinks £1.20, fresh juice £1.95.

Cambridge Blue

Omnivorous pub

85 Gwydir Street, Cambridge CB1 2LG (off Mill Road) Tel: 01223-471680
Open: Mon-Wed 12.00-14.30, 17.00-23.00; Thu-Sat 12.00-23.00, Sun 12.00-22.30.
Food: Mon-Fri 12.00-14.00, Sat-Sun -16.00; every evening 18.00-21.00.
www.the-cambridgeblue.co.uk
also on Facebook

Real ale community pub with a vegetarian menu . Baked potato and filling £4. 3 veggie mains £5 or £7 such as spicy butternut stew with chickpeas in and almonds, veg curry, pasta bake. Pitta with dips £4. Wine from £8 bottle, £2.50 glass. Truly staggering range of international bottled beers, listed on the website, or see Facebook for what's on today. Visa, MC.

Cambridge omni restaurants

Charlie Chan's
Omnivorous Chinese restaurant

14 Regent Street, Cambridge CB2 1DB
Tel: 01223-359 336
Open: every day 12.00-23.00

They offer a vegetarian set dinner, which includes soup and at least four different vegan dishes, and costs £16 per couple. Vegan desserts such as lychees £3. In the centre of town opposite Parker's Piece. Visa, MC. House wine £12.50 bottle, £3.25 glass.

Clowns
Omnivorous Italian cafe

54 King Street, Cambridge CB1 1LN
Tel: 01223-355711
Open: Mon-Sun 07.30-22.45

Veggie food and some vegan gnocchis and ratatouille. Locals say it's half the price of the Starbucks upstairs at Borders book store, and you get served much more quickly too. Licensed.

Efes
Omnivorous Turkish restaurant

78-80 King Street, Cambridge CB1 1LN
Tel: 01223-350491 or 500 005
Open: Mon-Fri 12.00-14.30, 18.00-23.00; Sat-Sun 12.00-23.00
www.restaurant-guide.com/efes-restaurant.htm

Lots of vegetarian mezze starters £3.95-5.50. House wine £12.90 bottle, glass £3.25. Children welcome, 2 high chairs. Visa, MC.

The Gardenia
Omnivorous Greek restaurant

2 Rose Crescent, Cambridge CB2 3LL
Tel: 01223-356 354
Open: every day 11.00-03.00
www.gardenia-restaurant.co.uk

Omnivorous Greek take-away and restaurant with lots of vegetarian and vegan food, such as falafel and hummous with pitta and salad £4.90. Mixed starters £5.90. Wine from £8 bottle, £2.90 glass. Tea and coffee from £1.50. Very popular with students.
Varsity Greek-Cypriot restaurant at 35 St Andrews Str CB2 3AR has a great vegetarian mezze plate and is very popular with students, tel: 01223-356060.

Mai Thai @ Hobbs Pavilion
Omnivorous Thai restaurant

Parkers Piece, Cambridge CB1 1JH
Tel: 01223-367 480
Open: every day 12.00-15.00, 17.30-23.00
www.mai-thai-restaurant.co.uk

15 vegetarian dishes £4.95-9.95. Platter of 6 vegetarian starters for 2, £6 per person, with spring rolls Set meal for at least two people £18.50 or £24 each which could include 5 starters, bean curd, mushroom, green curry, mixed veg stir-fry, steamed rice, aubergine, Thai salad and soup. House wine £15 for a bottle, £3.95 for a glass. Visa, MC, Amex. Reduction for students.

Pizza Express, Cambridge

Omnivorous Italian restaurant

7A Jesus Lane, Cambridge CB5 8BA
Tel: 01223-324 033
Open: Mon-Sun 11.30-23.00

26-28 Regent Street, City Centre, Cambridge CB2 1DB. Tel: 01223 306 777
Open: Mon-Sun 11.30-23.00
www.pizzaexpress.com

See Bedford for menu.

Cambridge shops

Al Amin

Oriental grocery shop and deli

100A-102A Mill Road, Cambridge CB1 2BD
Shop: 01223-576396
Clinic: 01223-566122
Open: Mon-Sat 9.00-19.30, Sun 10-19.00
www.al-amin.com

Wide selection of Asian foods including fresh tofu, spring rolls, red bean dumplings, mock duck, Bombay potatoes, pakoras and lots more.

Arjuna Wholefoods

Vegetarian co-operative shop

12 Mill Road, Cambridge CB1 2AD
Tel: 01223-364 845
Open: Mon-Sat 9.30-18.00, Sun closed
www.arjunawholefoods.co.uk
www.arjunahealth.co.uk. See cover photo.

Big range of wholefoods with a counter at the back with plenty of things for lunch including olive bread, pasta salads and houmous, all cooked upstairs by Mouth Music vegetarian catering company.
Loose organic fruit and veg, locally grown produce when possible More kinds of bread than we've ever seen in one wholefood store. Stacks of chilled and frozen including Cauldron, Redwood, Taifun, Dragonfly, Soyfoods, Tofutti, Wicken Fen, sprouts, pates, a dozen kinds of tofu, burgers, Swedish Glace, B'Nice, Booja Booja. Japanese foods. Herbs and spices.
Bodycare includes Faith in Nature, Weleda, Green People and Living Nature makeup. Women's personal care. Baby products. Essential oils.
Cleaning products include BioD and refills, Clearspring, Sodasan and Ecolino.
Remedies. Supplements by Viridian, Floradix, Nature's Own. Organic vegan wines and beers. Veggie dog food. Magazines.
Arjuna clinic upstairs at 12A offers various kinds of massage, counselling and psychotherapy, herbalism, kinesiology, NLP, pregnancy related therapies, reflexology, meditation using the Radiance Technique, baby massage, iridology, naturopathy, nutrition, Reiki, spiritual healing, tai chi.

Daily Bread Co-op

Vegetarian wholefood shop & cafe

Unit 3, Kilmaine Close, King's Hedges
Cambridge CB4 2PH (north side off A14)
Tel: 01223-423 177
Open: Mon 9.00-16.00, Tue-Sat 9.00-17.20, Sun closed (& Tue if bank holiday)
www.dailybread.co.uk

Workers cooperative run by a Christian group, to promote physical and spiritual health. Vegans will be especially delighted. They specialise in free-from just about anything products: soya, salt free, sugar, even carrageenan-free.
Coffee shop with hot drinks, cakes and biscuits, and you can buy prepared items in the shop to eat in the cafe.
The **shop** has lots of organic and local products with organic fruit and veg piled high Fridays and Saturdays. Organic local bread. Small deli section with a few salads, couscous, hummous,

salads, dips, gluten-free pies and pasties. Cakes including gluten-free and vegan. Redwood and Sheese, tofu, sausages, Provamel soya yogurts, Booja Booja and Swedish Glace non-dairy ice-cream. Vegan pestos and creams.
Carleys raw range of nut butters including tahini, apricot kernel, macademia all made in UK. *Rawr* vegan chocolate made in Cambridge. (see www.rawrchoc.com)
Lots of bodycare including Essential, Dead Sea Magik, Faith In Nature, Aubrey Organics. Natracare women's personal care and Mooncup. Baby things.
Cleaning products include Ecover with refills, and Suma Ecoleaf. Books on wholefood recipes, diet and trade issues that reflect the products.
Car park with recycling bins. Bring your own bags and boxes for shopping or buy one of their cloth shopping bags, they do not provide plastic carrier bags but can give you a cardboard box. Debit cards but no credit cards.

Cambridge shops

Holland & Barrett, Cambridge
Health food shop

6 Lion Yard, St Tibbs Row, Cambridge CB2 3ET. Tel: 01223-315603
Open: Mon-Sat 9-17.30, Sun 10.30-16.30

27 Fitzroy Street, Cambridge CB1 1ER
Tel: 01223-353524
Open: Mon-Sat 9-17.30, Sun 10.30-16.30

Lush, Cambridge
Vegetarian cosmetics & bodycare

4-5 Lion Yard, Cambridge CB2 3NA
Tel: 01223-352 881
Open: Mon-Fri 9.30-17.30, Wed till 19.30, Sat 9.30-18.00, Sun 11.00-17.00
www.lush.co.uk

Fun things to relax with in the bathroom of your B&B or at home such as foaming bath balls. Almost all products are vegan and clearly labelled as such.

Nasreen Dar
Indian supermarket

18-20 Histon Road (south end), Cambridge CB4 3LE. Tel: 01223-568 013
Open: Mon-Sat 08.00-20.00 Sun 08-14.00
www.nasreendar.com

Excellent shop selling nearly everything including lots of bags of pulses and fresh vegetable samosas, potato patties, battered aubergines and a fantastic range of frozen curries etc. They also have a take-away/deli section.

Revital Health @ Cambridge
Health food shop

5 Bridge Street (near the Round Church), Cambridge CB2 1UA. Tel: 01223-350433
Open: Mon-Sat 9.00-18.00, Sun 11-17.00
www.revital.co.uk

One of the largest Revital stores. Juice bar and fresh vegetarian food counter with sweet and savoury such as samosas, spring rolls, sausage rolls, date slices. Gluten-free foods. Vegan cheese, meat substitutes, Swedish Glaces, Booja Booja, B'Nice. Make your own peanut butter with their machine.
Beauty and skincare includes Dr Hauschka, Lavera, Weleda, Green People, Flint, Jason, Nature's Gate. MBT footwear.
Supplements, herbal and homeopathy. Some Ecover cleaning products. Organic wine, beer, ale and spirits. Wide range of health books. Previously known as Cambridge Health Foods.

Libra Aries Books
Alternative book shop

9 The Broadway, Mill Rd, Cambridge CB1 3AH
(between Cavendish Rd and Sedgwick St)
Tel: 01223-412 411
Open: Tue-Sat 10.30-18.00,
Sun-Mon closed
www.libra-aries-books.co.uk

Alternative bookshop with a section for new and secondhand vegan and vegetarian cookbooks. They stock the Vegan Society's bible of vegan nutrition *Plant Based Nutrition & Health* and this book!

Ely
Pizza Express, Ely
Omnivorous Italian restaurant

43 High Street, Ely CB7 4LF
Tel: 01353-665 999
Open: Mon-Sun 11.30-23.00
www.pizzaexpress.com

See Bedford for menu.

Hauxton
Organic Health
Omnivorous organic health food shop

87 Church Road, Hauxton CB22 5HS (3 miles south of Cambridge where A10 and M11 cross). Tel: 01223-870 101
Open:Tue-Sat 9-17.00, Thu til 18.30,
Sun-Mon closed
www.organichealth-cambridge.co.uk

Outstanding health food shop on the south side of Cambridge. It's in a nature reserve with a few chairs outside where you can relax with snacks and a cold drink after biking there. But some people come from all over the country and even abroad for their range of 3,000 product lines. Run since 1995 by a Green Party activist with a qualification in organic agriculture who used to work for Weleda and the Soil Association. Well worth a visit if you're in the region, you will be amazed by room after room of goodies.

Lots of organic fruit and veg. Organic breads from the local Cobs Bakery and Paul's Bakery. Sunnyvale vegan cakes. Vegan Christmas puddings and mince pies and Easter hot cross buns. Clive's pies. Vegan cheeses incldue Tofutti and Sheese. Big range of biodynamic Taifun flavoured tofu. Booja Booja ice-cream and truffles. Clearspring Japanese products.

Hard to find items such as rice squirty cream and mayo, heaps of vegan mayo's, wide range of Plamil products, Organica chocs. Big range of organic nut butters. Just Wholefoods vegan jelly crystals. Dairy-free, wheat-free, gluten-free, yeast-free foods that are Fairtrade and/or biodynamic. Yorkshire hemp flour, pancake mix. Quinoa and hazelnut milk. Local Fairfields Farm crisps from Suffolk and Cambridgeshire flour.

Bodycare includes Green People, Faith In Nature and refills, Jason, Aubrey Organics, Weleda, Yaoh. Handmade Norfolk soaps.

Ecover refills and BioD.

Homeopath in store and they sell Weleda remedies. Allergy testing. Alternative therapies clinic including allergy testing, naturopathy, Reiki, nutrition, Indian head massage, crystal healing, sports therapy, relexology etc.

Special diet cookbooks. Biodynamic gardening calendar. Mail order. Customer toilet.

Huntingdon

Pizza Express, Huntingdon
Omnivorous Italian restaurant

105 High Street, Huntingdon PE29 3LB
Tel: 01480-434 446
Open: Mon-Sun 11.30-23.00
www.pizzaexpress.com

See Bedford for menu.

Peterborough

Stop the Week
Vegetarian monthly meal

Drolma Buddhist Centre, Woodbyth, Dogsthorpe Road, Peterborough PE1 3PG
Tel: 01733-755444
Open: occasional Fridays 19.00-21.30
Centre open: daytime, best to phone first
www.drolmacentre.org.uk/stoptheweek.htm

A Friday night out with a difference, about once a month in the peaceful atmosphere of Drolma Kadampa (Mahayana) Buddhist Centre. See website for dates. The evening starts with a 20-minute relaxation meditation to help you unwind, followed by a 3-course vegetarian meal. £12. Book at least 24 hours in advance. Vegan/special diets give advance warning. You don't have to be Buddhist. Also meditation and Buddhism classes here and around the region, day courses, retreats, rooms to rent long-term.

Pizza Express, Peterborough
Omnivorous pizza restaurant

8A Cathedral Square, Peterborough, PE1 1XH
Tel: 01733-562984
Open: Mon-Sun 11.30-23.00
www.pizzaexpress.com

For menu see Bedford.

The Buddhist Centre (which doesn't have a cafe) tells us there's nowhere great for veggies in Peterborough, but you could also try Ask Pizza at 28-30 Priestgate, near the museum, open same hours as Pizza Express. There are also Indian restaurants where you can get the standard vegetable side dishes.

Peterborough Health Food Centre
Health food shop

25 The Arcade, Westgate, Peterborough PE1 1PY
Tel: 01733-566807
Open: Mon-Sat 9.00-17.30, Sun closed
www.peteroroughhealthfoods.co.uk

Organic foods, gluten and wheat-free products, dairy-free, diabetic foods. Fridge with pies, spring rolls, sos rolls, vegan cheeses and meat substitutes. No freezer. Gluten-free breads. Plamil vegan chocolate.
Bodycare, specialise in Weleda. Natracare. Baby things. Supplements include Solgar, Nature's Plus, Quest. Homeopathy and herbal medicines, flower remedies, essential oils. They can advise on local practitioners. Ecover cleaning products. Health books and magazines. MC, Visa.

Wisbech

Brian Hardy Ltd
Omnivorous organic health food shop

50 Hill Street, Wisbech PE13 1BD (between Peterborough and Kings Lynn on A47)
Tel: 01945-582437
Open: Mon-Fri 9-17.00, Sat 8.30-17.00, Sun closed.

One of the first health food shops in Britain, opened in 1961. Deli counter making fresh designer sandwiches and salads to order ("You design it, we make it"), brown rice, and they can grab

whatever you fancy from the shelves. Lots of bakery products. Fridge and freezer with vegan cheeses, soya yogurt, sausages and burgers, Swedish Glace.
All the leading brands of bodycare. Ecover cleaning products. Supplements, herbal and homeopathic remedies (also available by post). They can get in anything else you need. Allergy testing by appointment.

Chain Stores
Holland & Barrett
Health food shop

1 Coronation Parade, High St, **Ely** CB7 4LB
Tel: 01353-662330
Open: Mon-Sat 9.00-17.30, Sun 10-16.00

Unit G, Saint Benedicts, **Huntingdon** PE29 3PN
Tel: 01480-417203
Open: Mon-Sat 9.00-17.30, Sun closed

33 Long Causeway, **Peterborough** PE1 1YJ
Tel: 01733-311268
Open: Mon-Sat 9.00-17.30, Sun 10-17.00

Julian Graves
Health food shop

41 Bridge St, **Peterborough** PE1 1HA
Tel: 01733-891640
Open: Mon-Sat 9.00-17.30, Sun closed

The Cloisters, **Ely** CB7 4ZH
Tel: 01353-666633

Local group
Cambridge Vegans & Vegetarians

www.camvegans.xonline.org.uk

Informal collection of vegans and vegetarians of all ages from the Cambridge area who meet up regularly for food, events, and camaraderie. Meet at the Rainbow Bistro on the second Saturday of each month from 10:30 to midday or 1 depending on how many people turn up and how busy the Rainbow gets.

Catering
Mouth Music
Vegetarian caterers

12 Mill Road, Cambridge CB1 2AD
Tel: 07886 757987, 07732 113680
Open:Tues-Sat 9-17.00, Thu til 18.30
www.mouth-music.co.uk

Private functions, corporate lunches, product launches, wedding receptions, festivals or gourmet meals. They can arrange equipment hire and provide a relaxed professional staff for a memorable stress-free occasion. From £6.75 per head.

EAST Cambridgeshire

Next door to London but a world away, Essex has lively clubs, reasonably priced theatres, new cinemas, country walks, seaside towns, good shops, shopping malls, and if you know where to look there is some great vegetarian food to be had.

Our first choice for a veggie night out is **My Kitchen** in Leigh-on-Sea (Southend), a proper vegetarian restaurant with food from around the world. The main alternative is **A Pinch of Veg** in Ilford, a south Indian vegetarian restaurant. Saffron Walden has a brand new 99% vegetarian cafe called **Saffron** that is popular with local vegans. Elsewhere in the county we've listed restaurants recommended by readers such as My Kovalam or Pizza Express.

Tourism information: www.visitessex.com

25	Animal Sanctuary
25	Billericay
25	Braintree
26	Brentwood
26	Brightlingsea
26	Chelmsford
27	Clacton-on-Sea
28	Colchester
29	Dedham
30	Hockley, Ilford
31	Leigh-on-sea
32	Loughton
32	Manningtree
32	Romford
33	Saffron Walden
33	Southend
33	Upminster
34	Wickford
34	Wickham Bishops
34	Catering
35	Mail order
35	Local groups
36	Chain stores

Essex

Animal Sanctuary

Redwings Horse Sanctuary Ada Cole Rescue Centre

Horse sanctuary

Off the B181 in Broadley Common, near Nazeing in Essex EN9 2DH (near Harlow) Tel: 01508-481000
Open: all year daily 10.00-17.00 (last entry 16.30). Closed Xmas, Boxing Day and New Year's Day. Entry is free.
www.redwings.org.uk

In 2005 Redwings merged with the Ada Cole Memorial Stables in Essex, a rescue centre established in memory of an amazing lady who campaigned for animal welfare. You can meet more than 50 rescued horses, ponies, donkeys and mules at the site – some are permanent residents while others are looking for loving homes.

There are walking tours and horse care demos as well as a gift shop and information centre where you can adopt a pony, buy gifts or find out more about the horsey residents and the charity's welfare work.

Omnivorous cafe has vegetarian and vegan options, light refreshments including hot drinks and cakes.

Fully accessible to wheelchair users, with a concrete pathway through the middle of the site, WC and plenty of onsite parking. Dogs welcome on lead. Children's area. Birthday parties. Entry is free. Other centres in Norfolk (page 62) and Warwickshire.

Billericay

Nature's Table

Health food shop

8 The Walk, 128 High Street, Billericay CM12 9YB. Tel: 01277-655 444
Open: Mon-Sat 9.00-17.00

Small health food shop stocking the usual packaged staples. Fridge (but no freezer) with Sheese, meat substitutes, soya yogurt. Bodycare. Cleaning products.

For eating out in Billericay try **Yau's** (Chinese) 5 High Street CM12 9BE, Tel 01277-652 488; or **Gandhi** (Indian) at 3 Holly Court, High Street CM12 9AP Tel 01277-652 141.

Braintree

Pizza Express, Braintree

Omnivorous pizza restaurant

R1 Freeport Designer Shopping Village, Charter Way, Braintree, Essex CM77 8YH
Tel: 01376-528 789
Open: Sun-Thu 11.30-23.00, Fri-Sat -23.30
www.pizzaexpress.com

See Brentwood branch for details. Separate bar. Outside dining.

The Natural Way

Health food shop

14 New Street, Braintree CM7 1ES
Tel: 01376-329009
Open: Mon-Sat 9.00-17.30, Wed & Sat from 08.30. Sun closed.
www.thenaturalway.co.uk

The fridge has take-away savouries such as spring rolls, vegan shepherd's pie, spiced pasties, apricot and date slices. Organic fruit & veg and deliveries to surrounding areas. Frozen and chilled with sos rolls, vegan cheese, ice-cream, yoghurt, Fry's, Goodlife, Realeat, Linda McCartney, Booja Booja and Swedish Glace ice- and B'Nice rice-cream. Wheat-free pasta and cereals. Bodycare. Baby food and bodycare, nappies. Supplements include Quest, FSC, Viridian, Solgar, Kordels. Sports nutrition. Aromatherapy. Weleda homeopathy. A. Vogel tinctures. Ecover refills, Method and Enviroclean. Books.

Brentwood

Pizza Express

Omnivorous pizza restaurant

5 High Street, Brentwood CM14 4RG (by the double roundabout)
Tel: 01277-233 569
Open: Mon-Sun 11.30-24.00
www.pizzaexpress.com

Pizza chain that can make vegan pizzas. You ask them to leave off the cheese and they can manage to do this. They also do salads. Vegetarian options include margharita, giardinera, mushroom and Veneziana. Live jazz Tue 19.30-22.30. Popular with children, baby changing facilities. For more details see Bedford.

Brightlingsea

Kovalam, Brightlingsea

Omnivorous South Indian restaurant

27 Waterside, Brightlingsea CO7 0AY
Tel: 01206-305555
Open: every day 12.00-14.30 (not Fri), 18.00-23.00 (Fri, Sat 24.00)

Sister to My Keralam in Ipswich (see Suffolk) which is popular with veggies there, with a similar menu. Veg platter of starters £8.95 for two people. Dosas £5.45, curries around £3.95 per dish, pooris and iddlis £4.95. They tell us the gulab jamun is vegan £2.25.
House wine £9.75 bottle, £2.25 glass. Children welcome, high chair. MC, Visa. Another branch in Clacton.

Cornflower Wholefoods

Vegetarian wholefood shop

49 High Street, Brightlingsea, Essex CO7 0AQ
Tel: 01206-306679
Open: Mon-Sat 9.00-17.00, Sun closed
www.healthyone.co.uk

Chilled has things like pasties, bean salads, non-dairy cheeses, meat substitutes. Full range of Swedish Glace and B'Nice rice-cream. Organic fruit and veg. Bread. Lots of gluten-free foods. Bodycare includes Jason, Faith In Nature, Dead Sea Magik, Organic Children's from Green People and others. Women's personal care. Ecover, BioD and Clearspring cleaning products. Supplements. Homeopathy (they make their own), remedies, aromatherapy. Homeopath in store. They can get stuff in if you want it, e.g. baby things.

Chelmsford

Cosmoflame

Omnivorous Mediterranean restaurant

8-10 Broomsfield Rd, Chelmsford CM1 1SN
Tel: 01245-493 929. Bookings and enquiries out of hours: 07802 290288
Open: Mon-Sat, 11.30-14.30, 17.30-22.30 (kitchen closes); Fri-Sat 23.00, Sun closed
www.cosmoflame.co.uk

Lots of Greek, Turkish and Italian dishes. Cold starters include hummous, vine leaves stuffed with rice and pine kernels, salads, fried aubergine and veg cube, pasta, £2.50-£3, pasta tricolore £4.50. Some hot starters £3 such as chargrilled aubergines, peppers. Mixed starters £7. Mains such as stuffed aubergine moussaka £9.50 (can be without cheese), large portion of stuffed vine leaves £7.50, broad bean and chickpea falafel £7.50. Children can have a small starter such as melon then a rice or pasta dish and dessert £5.50.

House wine £12.95, glass £2.95. Organic produce used whenever possible. Vegan desserts £3.50-4.50 include some baklava, some vegan, crostata noci e fichi (shortcrust pastry with walnuts and figs). Also take-away. Check website for latest menu and opening times. Previously Italian restaurant called Cosmopolitan, now with more variety of Mediterranean dishes but same owner who is keen to attract veggies and vegans. MC, Visa.

Pizza Express, Chelmsford

Omnivorous pizza restaurant

219 Moulsham Street, Chelmsford CM2 0LR
Tel: 01245-491 466
Open: Sun-Thu 11.30-23.00, Fri-Sat -24.00
www.pizzaexpress.com

See Brentwood branch for details. Outside dining. Baby changing. Near the cathedral. For menu see Bedford.

Lanthai

Omni Thai restaurant & take-away

11-12 Victoria Rd, Chelmsford CM1 1NY
Tel: 01245-290600
Open: Mon-Sat 12.00-14.30
Mon-Sun 18.00-23.30, closed Sun lunch
www.lanthai.co.uk

Recommended by Gibsons as the owner's wife here is vegetarian and they really know what we like. Ask for Monring Glory veg with no fish sauce. beancurd dishes, stir-fries or curries £6.85, steamed (coconut) rice £2.75, fried rice noodles with broccoli £4.75. 2 course dinner Mon-Thu from £10. Free delivery within 3 miles over £20. Licensed. Beer patio.

Gibsons Cornershop & Deli

Convenience store, deli & off-licence

222 Rainsford Road, Chelmsford. CM1 2PD
Tel: 01245-354525
Open: Mon-Fri 07.30-21.00,
Sat 8.30-21.00, Sun 9.00-21.00

Local independent shop owned by a vegan, a veggie and an omnivore. Some fruit and veg. Bread. Fridge and freezer with Delphi lentil and chickpea salads in summer, tofu, tofu sausages, vegan cheese, soya spread, olives, Realeat Vegemince, burgers, rashers, Linda McCartney, Fry's, Swedish Glace (and cornets in summer), B'Nice rice cream. Vegan chocolate by Plamil, Organica, Humdinger. They don't sell wholefoods apart from soya milk, organic pasta and brown rice, but can order stuff in for you. Usual offie drinks, some vegan wines, beers and organic pear and apple cider.

Watch out if you're driving, Mon-Sat 2 to 3pm it's residents' parking only out front, no restrictions Sunday. MC, Visa.

Clacton-on-Sea

Kovalam, Clacton

Omnivorous South Indian restaurant

3 Rosemary Rd, Clacton-on-Sea CO15 1NY
Tel: 01255-470444
Open: Tue-Sun 12.00-15.00, 18.00-23.00, Fri-Sun 24.00, Mon closed.

SIster restaurant of Kovalam in Brightlingsea and My Keralam in Ipswich (Suffolk) with similar menu. Dosas from £2.95, most items £4.95-5.95. No vegan desserts. This branch does not have alcohol, but you can bring your own. Children welcome, no high chair. MC, Visa.

EAST Essex

Clacton-on-Sea

Pizza Express, Clacton

Omnivorous pizza restaurant

2 Marine Parade West, Clacton on Sea
CO15 1RH. Tel: 01255-423248
Open: Mon-Sun 11.30-22.00
www.pizzaexpress.com

See Bedford for menus.

All Natural

Health food shop

58A Rosemary Rd, Clacton-on-Sea
CO15 1PA. Tel: 01255-435629
Open: Mon-Sat 9.00-17.00, Sun closed

Fridge with no take-away, but they do have vegan cheeses. Bodycare includes Faith In Nature and Jason. Ecover clearning products. Women's personal care. Supplements. Homeopathy, remedies, aromatherapy. Health and recipe books. They can order in whatever you want.

Upstairs are therapy rooms offering by appointment relexology, homeopathy, sports massage, hypnotherapy.

Avalon Natural Health & Therapy Centre

Health food shop

6 St. John's Road, Great Clacton,
Clacton-on-Sea CO15 4BP
Tel: 01255-436 059
Open: Mon-Fri 9.00-17.00, Sat-Sun closed
www.avalonhealthcentre.co.uk

They don't sell food but do have a large range of dried herbs and supplements. Small range of teas and toothpaste. Homeopathic and Bach remedies. Some books.

Treatments available are acupuncture, allergy testing, chiropody, counselling, homeopathy, hypnotherapy, herbal medicine, iridology, massage, naturopathy, reflexology. Free consultations with regard to general health problems are available on request, subject to practitioner availability. Wheelchair access. Also an acupuncture clinic at nearby Frinton-on-Sea.

Colchester

LevelBest ArtCafe

Vegetarian cafe

D'arcy House, 3 Culver Street East, Colchester CO1 1LD (behind Natural History Museum)
Tel: 01206-366059
Open: Mon-Fri 9.30-15.30, closed bank holidays and 10 days Christmas-New Year
www.dacontrust.co.uk

Great value vegetarian Fairtrade cafe in arts centre and gallery in a grade 2 listed building, run by the Dacon Trust to provide work training to people with learning disabilities. Soup £2 with gluten-free homemade rolls. Vegan spicy bean casserole with jacket potato or side salad £2.50. Muffins £1. Cakes £1 slice but not vegan. Cookies 20p. Fairtrade filter coffee, teas and herb teas £1. Bottled water 50p per glass.

Chef Canton

Chinese restaurant & take-away

2A Crouch Street, Colchester CO3
Tel: 01206-572 703
Open: Mon-Sat 12.30-13.45, 17.30-22.30, closed Sun lunch

Set vegetarian meal £12.50 each, minimum two people. Wine £3.05 glass, £11.95 bottle. Beer £3. Children welcome, under 4'7" half price. MC, Visa.

China Chef
Chinese restaurant & take-away

73 Crouch Street, Colchester CO3 3EZ
Tel: 01206-546 953
Lunch: Mon-Fri 12-14.00, Sat-Sun closed;
Eve: Mon-Sun 17.30 23.00 (Fri-Sat till 23.30)
www.china-chef.co.uk

Lunch menu includes mixed veg curry with noodles £6.95 or Szechuan hot and sour mxed veg with steamed rice £6.50. A la carte dishes £4.20-5.70. Set vegetarian dinner for two people £10.70 each take-away, eat in £12.50. House wine £11.90 bottle, £3.10 glass. Children welcome. MC, Visa.

Pizza Express, Colchester
Omnivorous pizza restaurant

1 St Runwald's Street, Colchester CO1 1HP (off the High Street behind the Town Hall)
Tel: 01206-760 680
Open: Sun-Thu 11.30-23.00, Fri-Sat -24.00
www.pizzaexpress.com

See Bedford branch for menu. Life jazz Tuesdays. Baby changing.

The Natural Food Shop
Vegetarian health food shop

27 Sir Issacs Walk, Colchester CO1 1JJ
Tel: 01206-542 844
Open: Mon-Tue, Sat 9.00-17.30;
Wed-Fri 9.30-17.30; Sun closed
www.thenaturalfoodshop.co.uk

Organic and Fairtrade foods. Chilled and frozen includes vegan cheeses, tofu, meat substitutes, Swedish Glace, B'Nice and Booja Booja. Lots of bodycare including Green People, Faith In Nature, Jason, Lavera, Barefoot Botanicals. Children's bodycare. Natural hair dye. Baby organics.
Ecover refills, BioD, Clearspring cleaning. Supplements include Solgar, Quest, Solarary, Nelson, Life Plan, Nature's Plus, Nature's Aid, Nature's Own, Bio Force. Sports nutrition. Herbal, homeopathy, Bach flower. Health books. They can direct you to local practitioners.

Sante
Vegetarian health food shop

14 Trinity Street, Colchester CO1 1JN
Tel: 01206-548080
Open: Mon-Sat 9.30-17.30, Sun closed

They don't sell much food but there are raw specialities from detoxyourworld such as macca, cacao powder, agave, chocolate bars. Bodycare includes Dr Haushka, Jason, Weleda, Barefoot Botanicals, Lavera, Green People. Pukka, Vogel, Higher Nature, Helio and Viridian supplements. Absolute Aromas. Homeopathy. Crystal Herbs local company Bach handmade Bach flower remedies. There are therapies on site and advice. The owner Natasha has a degree in complementary medicine and does homeopathy, including for pregnancy and children. Staff know Reiki, massage and Alicia (Dr Hauschka), and they have the UK's only energy enhancement system for deep relaxation.

Dedham

Dedham Centre Tea Room
Vegetarian tea rooms

Arts & Crafts Centre, High Street, Dedham CO7 6AD. Tel: 01206-322 677
Open: Mon-Sun10-17.00 except 24-6 Dec
www.dedhamartandcraftcentre.co.uk

Now open 25 years. Being just off the A12, this is a popular pitstop for people driving up to Norfolk. It's also popular with walkers going to Flatford Mill along the river where Constable used to paint, and the Alfred Munnings museum.

Light lunches, £3.25 for soup with bread, lots of salads £5.25 or £6.50 with jacket potato. Main meals with salad from £6.85. They have some vegan regulars but need to know in advance if you want something special. Tea and coffee £1.20. Free car park in the village. Children welcome, high chairs but not baby changing. You can park your dog outside and they will provide water. No credit cards.

Hockley

The Shadhona

Omnivorous Indian restaurant

200 Main Road, Hawkwell, Hockley SS5 4EH
Tel: 01702-207 188
Train: Hockley BR
Open: every day 12.30-14.30, 18.00-23.00 inc. bank holidays, closed 25-6 Dec

Around 6 veggie main dishes £4.95 such as veg masala, korma, passanda (cooked with white wine), dhansak, korai (cooked in a flaming pot in a thick spicy sauce) and 14 side dishes £2.75. House wine £11.95 bottle, glass £2.95. Children welcome, it's a family restaurant. MC, Visa.

Sunrise Natural Health

Health food shop & clinic

31 Spa Road, Hockley SS5 4AZ
Tel: 01702-207 017
Open: Mon-Sat 9.00-17.00, Wed till 19.00
www.sunrisehealth.co.uk

2,000 products in the shop, particularly popular with people with allergies, diabetes etc. Vegan cheese and yoghurt, Swedish Glace andB'Nice rice cream. Vegan cookies and cakes.
Lots of bodycare includes Faith In Nature, Optima Australian tea tree products. 600 kinds of supplements including Biocare, Lamberts and Solgar,
Bioforce, Quest, Nature's Aid. Herbal and homeopathy. Natracare women's personal care. Ecover refills. They specialise in ordering in anything else you need.
Clinic with acupuncture, aromatherapy and massage, chiropody and podiatry, cholesterol and blood glucose testing, nutrition and diet, homeopathy, hypnotherapy, medical herbalism, osteopathy, reflexology.

Ilford

A Pinch of Veg

Vegetarian South Indian restaurant

751-753 High Rd, Seven Kings, Essex IG3 8RN. (between Spencer Rd & Westwood Rd) Tel: 020-8590 0644
Train: Seven Kings, Goodmayes BR
Tube: Newbury Park
Open: Mon-Sun 12.00-23.00
www.apinchofveg.com (menus)

Indian, Italian and Oriental dishes, no eggs. Open kitchen. Starters £1.50-£3.60 such as samosa, bhel puri, onion spinach bhajia, piri piri or Hong Kong cassava, mushroom bruschetta, spring roll, tempura veg with daikon; mixed starters platter for two £4.50. Main dishes come in two sizes from £2.20 to £5.50 and include dosas, pizza, penne arrabiata with broccoli and green beans, conchiglie napolitana with courgettes and mushrooms, noodle dishes, 5-spice rice with veg, aloo gobi, karahi dhingri hot veg. Standard naan 90p is without butter, basmati rice £1.50, wheat noodles £1.60.
Set Indian, Italian or Chinese lunch £5.95 served in a Japanese style bento box with starter, main, extras and drink. Desserts £2.40-3.50 include sorbets, Chinese toffee apple.
Soft drinks and freshly squeezed juices £1.50-£2.20. Wine from £8.95 bottle, £2.60 glass. Indian, Italian and Chinese

beer £2.40. Chai and coffees £1.20-1.50, green tea free.

Health Mantra
Health food shop

75 Cranbrook Road, Ilford IG1 4PG
Shop: 020-8514 4443
Mail order: 0800 043 1475
Open: Mon-Sat 9.30-18.30, Sun 11.30-15.30
www.healthmantra.co.uk

As well as organic and Fairtrade foods, they have bread. chilled and frozen fake meats, non-dairy cheeses and Tofutti vegan ice-cream.
Bodycare includes Jason, Faith In Nature, Alva, Weleda, Green People, Desert Essence, Avalon. Natracare oganic women's personal care and hair colours. Weleda, Earth Friendly, Green People and Earth's Best babycare. Ecover and Faith In Nature cleaning products.
Supplements include Solgar, Nature's Plus, Viridian, Biocare, Higher Nature and Quest. Pukka herbal remedies, Weleda and Ainsworth homeopathy. From August 2009 they are starting complementary therapies on the premises. Lots of books on health, vegan and gluten-free cooking.

Leigh-on-Sea (Southend)
My Kitchen
Vegetarian restaurant

80 Leigh Road, Leigh-on-Sea SS9 1BZ
Tel: 01702-719 222
Open: Tue- 12-16.00, Wed-Fri 12-22.00 Sat 10-22.00, Sun 9-16.00, Mon closed
www.mykitchen.org.uk

Menu changes daily. Everything homemade. Formerly Pulse vegetarian cafe and still run by the original Pulse chef. They use locally grown produce with many seasonal, organic ingredients from local farms, and try to stay away from stereotypical vegetarian fare but do veggie versions of traditional worldwide dishes.
Brunch £4.50 such as sauteed potatoes with asparagus. Lunchtime mains £7.50 such as sweet potato and borlotti bean pie; pie and mash. They make their own vegan sausages with beans, red onion gravy and garlic mash.
Wed and Thursday nights they do a 10 dish tapas style menu £10.50 per person for the lot. Fri-Sat nights starters £4, mains £8.50. Sun big breakfast £7 with unlimited juice, tea or coffee and the papers. Sun lunch £15 for 3 courses. Fairtrade organic coffee £1.80, teas £1.40. Juices and smoothies £2 during the day. Essex organic house wine £12.95 bottle, glass £3.40.
Children welcome, high chairs. MC, Visa. A couple of outside tables.
Books, leaflets. Outside catering all events.

Greens Health Foods
Health food shop

37 Rectory Grove, Leigh-on-Sea SS9 2HA
Tel: 01702-475338
Open: Mon-Sat 8.30-17.30, Sun closed
chrisgreen@hotmail.com

Big range of foods. Fridge has vegan cheeses, Redwood, yoghurt, Swedish Glace, B'Nice, Fry's. Village Bakery bread. Bodycare includes Desert Essence, Green People, Faith in Nature, Suma soaps. Women's personal care. Baby things. Ecover refills. Homeopathy, herbal. Aromatherapy. Sometimes magazines. One of the staff is a qualified nutritionist.

Leigh-on-Sea (Southend)
The Vitamin Service
Health food shop

8 Madeira Avenue, Leigh-on-Sea SS9 3EB
Tel: 01702-470 923, 0800-652 7855
Open: Mon-Fri 9-16.00
www.thevitaminservice.com

Postal service for supplements and a shop for locals to call in. A few books.

Loughton
Pizza Express, Loughton
Omnivorous pizza restaurant

281-283 High Road, Loughton IG10 1AH
Tel: 020-8508 3303
Open: Mon-Sat 11.30-23.00, Sun -22.30
www.pizzaexpress.com

See Bedford branch for details. Outside dining. Baby changing.

Manningtree
The Wholefood Store
Wholefood shop

26 High Street, Manningtree CO11 1AJ
Tel: 01206-391200
Open: Mon-Fri 9.00-18.00, Sat 8.30-17.00, Sun closed
www.the-wholefoodstore.co.uk

Big family run store a short stroll from the banks of the Stour Estuary, on the Essex/Suffolk border. 2000 wholefoods, half organic. They bag up in cellophane bags so you can buy a sack of something if you want. Organic fruit and veg, much of it local. Dairy, gluten-free, Fairtrade, macrobiotic. Lots of Asian foods. Baked goods delivered twice a week from the Metfield Bakery. Fridge with pastries, vegan salads, burritos, dolmades, hummous, vegan cheeses and meat substitutes. Freezer with samosas, burritos, Frys/Beanies, nut cutlets, falafels, veg, fruit, Tofutti, Swedish Glace and Booja Booja.
Booja Booja truffles, Montezuma, Organica, Divine, Plamil and Conscious raw vegan chocolate. Lots of raw food bars.
Bodycare includes Dr Hauschka, Barefoot Botanicals, Weleda, Lavera, Green People, Jason and Dr Bronners, Natracare.
Supplements include Viridian, Solaray, Vega, Higher Nature and Nature's Aid. Herbal medicines, Pukka herbs, Vogel tinctures, homeopathy, Crystal Herbs.
BioD, Earth Friendly, Clearspring, Ecover and refills, chlorine free bleach, recycled toilet paper, lots of baby stuff. Unbleached parchment paper and baking cups, recycled aluminium foil. Water filters, biodegradable bin liners, sandwich bags. Eco-friendly Indian newspaper bags.
MC, Visa.

Romford
Pizza Express, Romford
Omnivorous pizza restaurant

The Brewery, Romford RM1 1AU
Tel: 01708-725 690
Open: Mon-Sat 11.30-23.00, Sun -22.00
www.pizzaexpress.com

See Bedford branch for details. Outside dining. Live music. Baby changing.

GNC
Health food shop

16N Laurie Walk, Liberty Shopping Centre
Romford RM1 3RT. Tel: 01708-747 192
Open: Mon-Sat 9-17.30, Sun 10.30-16.30

Stocks vegetarian capsules, supplements especially bodybuilding, and snack bars. Holland & Barrett next door. (see end of this chapter)

Saffron Walden
Saffron
99% vegetarian wholefood cafe

52 High Street, Saffron Walden CB10 1EE
Tel: 01799-527833
Open: Mon-Fri 9.00-17.00, Sat 9.00-16.00, Sun closed
www.saffron-cafe.co.uk

Opened May 2009, all veggie except for a bacon roll. It is fantastic to see such a place open up around here, as the only other vegetarian place in the near vicinity is Rainbow in Cambridge. They cater well for vegans and gluten-free diets.

Snacky things like toast, toasted teacakes, parsnip crisps and hummous dips. Vegan carrot pancake with salad and hummous £5.50. Soup with granary bread £3.75. Baked potatoes with fillings £5.50. Main course salads £6.

Hot and cold sandwiches and panini £3.50-3.75 such as falafel, roast veg, lots of chutneys.

Unusual cakes, some vegan and gluten-free, such as apple and date or coconut and banana £2.50, can be served with soya cream.

Milkshakes and fresh fruit smoothies £1.50 small, £2.50 large (nearly a pint). Lots of pots of teas £1.30, with herbal made from actual herbs rather than a bag. Coffee £1.30; cappuccino, latte, hot choc £1.60-1.80. Soya milk available.

Children's portions, high chairs, can heat up baby food for you. Dogs welcome outside, they have a dog bowl. 2 outside tables. Take-away available. Cash and cheque only.

They sell lots of herbs and spices by the ounce, candles, hand-made cards, fruit vinegars, olive oil, Organic Meltdown Fairtrade chocolates, locally grown Walden vegetables (some organic), unusual gifts such as oil burners.

Southend on Sea
Pizza Express, Southend
Omnivorous pizza restaurant

9 London Road, Southend-on-Sea SS1 1PR
Tel: 01702-435 585
Open: Mon-Sat 11.30-23.00, Sun 12-22.30
www.pizzaexpress.com

See Bedford branch for details.
For Southend see also Leigh-on-Sea.

Upminster
Pizza Express, Upminster
Omnivorous pizza restaurant

131-3 St Mary's Lane, Upminster RM14 2SH
Tel: 01708-224 111
Open: Mon-Sun 11.30-23.00, Sun 12-22.00
www.pizzaexpress.com

See Bedford branch for details.

Amethyst Healthlines
Health food shop

32 Corbets Tey Road, Upminster RM14 2AD
Tel: 01708-220 495
Open: Mon-Sat 10-17.30, Wed -13.00

Organic food. Solgar supplements. Herbal remedies. Reflexology and aromatherapy available on the premises.

Waltham Abbey
Abbey Health Foods
Health food shop

3 Sun Street, Waltham Abbey EN9 1ER
Tel: 01992-650 014
Open: Mon-Wed, Fri-Sat 9-13.00, 14-17.00. Thu closed.

Owner is a qualified nutritional therapist and happy to advise. Most products are vegetarian. Chiller and freezer with oils,

EAST Essex

drinks, superfoods, vegan cheeses, Swedish Glace. Bodycare including Aubrey Organics, Optima, Nature's Response, Bioetica, Grandma Vines, ESI, Vogel, Absalom hair growth enhancer, Hope's Cream, Weleda. Ecover. Big range of supplements include Vogel, Nature's Aid, Healthsense, FSC, Lifeplan, Solaray, Ortis, Nature's Plus, All Seasons. Aromatherapy. Weleda homeopathy and some Ainsworth. The staff are all qualified or training in nutrition, naturopathy, personal fitness, weight management or homeopathy and they have a clinic room with various practictioners.

Wickford
Wickford Health Store
Health food shop

Unit 7, Ladygate Centre, High Street, Wickford SS12 9AZ. Tel: 01268-733710
Open: Mon-Fri 9.00-17.30, Sat 9.00-17.00, Sun closed
www.wickfordhealthstore.co.uk
www.keepmewell.co.uk

Moved into new premises summer 2009. Fridge and freezer with non-dairy cheese, yogurt, meat substitutes, Swedish Glace, Booja Booja, and they may start doing lunchy things.
Bodycare includes Faith In Nature, Jason, Weleda, Thursday Plantation. Women's personal care. Baby bodycare.
Supplements include Solgar, Quest, Lifeplan, Nature's Aid, Bioforce, Lamberts, Biocare. Sports nutrition. Homeopathy and remedies.
Ecover clearning products.
The associated Centre for Natural Health is nearby with reflexology, acupuncture, pilates, yoga, cranial and body massage, Reiki, shiatsu, psychic healing, osteopathy, homeopathy, allergy testing (also in the shop). 14-16 The Broadway, Wickford SS11 7AA. . 01268-451663.

Wickham Bishops
Wickham Bishops Health Foods
Health food shop

12 The Street, Wickham Bishops CM8 3NN
Tel: 01621-890004
Open: Mon-Sat 9.00-17.30, Sun closed
www.wickhambishopshealthfoods.co.uk

Fridge and freezer, dairy-free cheeses, soya yogurt, meat substitutes, Swedish Glace, Tofutti, B'Nice rice-cream. You can pick up hummous and 3-bean salads and cooked sausages for a picnic lunch. Organic foods. Dairy-free and gluten-free. They specialise in foods for all allergy sufferers. Can order in special breads.
Bodycare includes Jason, Avalon, Faith In Nature, Tisserand, Weleda, Dead Sea Magik, Barefoot Botanicals. Naturtint hair colouring. Women's personal care. Weleda and Green People baby things.
Supplements include Viridian, Nature's Aid, Quest, Solgar, Bioforce, Biocare, Solaray, Kordels. Weleda and New Era homeopathy and remedies, Bach flower. Detox and weight management supplies. Sports nutrition. Aromatherapy. They can order anything else you want. Books.

Catering
Leon's Vegetarian Catering
Gourmet vegetarian catering

132b London Road, Brentwood CM14 4NS
Tel: 01277-218 661
leonsveg@aol.com. www.leonlewis.co.uk

Mouthwatering vegetarian and vegan catering, buffets, cookery demonstrations, any event nationwide. Amazing fungus forays in the woods in autumn and late spring followed by cooking the booty and quaffing from Leon's extensive wine cellar.

Mail Order
Spiralseed
Vegan books and permaculture

www.spiralseed.co.uk

Vegan, ethical initiative based in Essex. Earthright books, posters and T-shirts, forest gardening, permaculture design, consultancy and teaching. Books for young green vegans.

Local Groups
NESX Vegans

www.nesxvegans.makessense.co.uk
nesxvegans@hotmail.co.uk Jill Adams

Social and active group for vegans and vegetarians in north-east Essex, based in Colchester.

Southend Animal Aid

www.myspace.com/southendanimalaid

VeggieVision
Internet TV station

www.veggievision.tv

Founded by Essex's leading vegan entrepreneur, vegangelist, writer, tv and radio presenter Karin Ridgers, featuring reports, cookery videos and interviews with vegans and celebrities including Jodie Marsh, Benjamin Zephaniah and Jerome Flynn.

mad promotions
Vegan PR agency

Independent House, Radford Business Centre, Radford Way, Billericay CM12 0BZ
Tel: 01277-653603
www.mad-promotions.com

PR for veggie businesses that are Making a Difference. Passionate about promoting veggie stuff and getting the right people into the media. Quote Vegetarian Guides for special offer.

EAST Essex

Vegetarian Guides make great presents
Guides to London, Britain, Europe, the world
www.vegetarianguides.co.uk

Essex chain stores
Holland & Barrett
Health food shop

49 East Street, **Barking** IG11 8EJ
Tel: 020-8591 8017

51A Eastgate Centre, **Basildon** SS14 1AE
Tel: 01268-285098
Open: Mon-Sat 9.00-17.30, Sun 10-16.00

58 High Street, **Billericay** CM12 9BS
Tel: 01277-634980

40 Bank Street, **Braintree** CM7 1UR
Tel: 01376-567696

Unit 17 The Bay Tree Centre, **Brentwood** CM14 4BX. Tel: 01277-359 891

4-5 Exchange Way, **Chelmsford** CM1 1XB
Tel: 01245-258 748
Open: Mon-Sat 9.00-17.30, Sun 10-16.00

11 Station Rd, **Clacton-on-Sea** CO15 1TD
Tel: 01255-435551

8 Pelhams Lane, **Colchester** CO1 1JT
Tel: 01206-546 009
Open: Mon-Sat 9.00-17.30, Sun closed

5 Priory Walk, **Colchester** CO1 1LG
Tel: 01206-369129
Open: Mon-Sat 9.00-17.30, Sun closed

259 High Street, **Epping** CM16 4BP
Tel: 01992-572051

6 Grays Town Centre, **Grays** RM17 6QE
Tel: 01375-387357

11 Broad Walk, **Harlow** CM20 1HX
Tel: 01279-425543
Open: Mon-Sat 9.00-17.30, Sun 10-16.00

52 Cranbrook Rd, **Ilford** IG1 4PG
Tel: 020-8553 2808

Unit 250, **Lakeside** Shop Ctr, Grays RM20 2XP
Tel: 01708-869226
Open: Mon-Fri 10-22.00, Sat 9.00-21.00, Sun 11.00-17.00

212 High Rd, **Loughton** IG10 1DZ
Tel: 0208-5321163

55 High Street, **Rayleigh** SS6 7EW
Tel: 01268-779249

Unit 17, Laurie Walk, **Romford** RM1 3RT
Tel: 01708-722349
Open: Mon-Sat 9-18.00, Sun 10.30-16.30

25 King St, **Saffron Walden** CB10 3EU
Tel: 01799-516736
Open: Mon-Sat 9.00-17.30, Sun closed

185-7 High Street, **Southend** SS1 1LL
Tel: 01702-338356
Open: Mon-Sat 9.00-17.30, Sun 10-16.00

Unit 6, The Grove Shopping Centre, **Witham** CM8 2YT. Tel: 01376 520145

Redwings Horse Sanctuary, Ada Cole Visitor Centre, page 25

Berkhamstead	38
Bishops Stortford	38
Harpenden	38
Hatfield	39
Hemel Hempstead	39
Hertford	40
Heydon	40
Hitchin	41
Kings Langley	42
Letchworth Garden City	42
Potters Bar	42
Radlett	43
Rickmansworth	43
Sawbridgeworth	43
St. Albans	43
Stevenage	44
Tring	44
Ware	45
Watford	45
Welwyn Garden City	46
Chain stores	47
Local group	47
Curry delivery	47

Hertfordshire

Berkhamstead

Pizza Express, Berkhamstead
Omnivorous pizza chain

350 High Street, Berkhamsted HP4 1HT
Tel: 01442-879 966
Open: Mon 11:30-22:00.,
Tue-Wed & Sun 11:30- 22:30pm,
Thu-Sat 11:30-23:00
www.pizzaexpress.co.uk (menus)

For menu see Bedford. Meeting room. Baby changing. Children's parties.

Cook's Delight
Vegetarian and vegan organic & biodynamic food shop

360-364 High Street, Berkhamsted HP4 1HU
Tel: 01442-863584
Open: Mon-Tu 10.00-17.00,
Fri 10.00-19.00, Sat 10.00-18.00
www.cooksdelight.co.uk

Everything in this shop is organic and they don't sell anything remotely dodgy. 4500 certified organic food and drink lines from small farms, organisations and workers' co-ops, most of it vegan. Fruit and veg. Chilled includes Clive's pies, Viana and Taifun tofu. Vegan organic and biodynamic wines, beers, cider, spirits and juices. Very much into organic macrobiotic including miso, tempeh, tofu, sea vegetables, daikon and burdock in season. All Natural handmade sourdough bread from Cambridge delivered Thursday.
Bodycare includes Essential, Dr Bronner, Faith In Nature, Organic Botanics, Druide. Urtekram and Green People toothpaste without sodium lauryl suphate. Natracare women's personal care. Maltox nappies. BioD, Sonnett and Ecos cleaning products.
The whole range of Nature's Answer organic vegan remedies, mostly alcohol-free. Colloidal minerals.
Box scheme covering Herts, Beds and Bucks and also Manchester, Leeds, Bristol and Bath.

Bishops Stortford

The Natural Way
Health food shop

15 Florence Walk, Bishops Stortford CM23 2NZ. Tel: 01279-465850
Open: Mon-Sat 9.00-17.30, Sun closed
www.thenaturalway.co.uk
organic-delivery.co.uk

Organic fruit & veg and deliveries to surrounding areas. Wheat-free pasta and cereals. Frozen and chilled with sos rolls; vegan cheese, yogurt and ice-cream; Fry's, Goodlife, Realeat, Linda McCartney; Booja Booja and Swedish Glace ice- and B'Nice rice-cream. Bodycare. Baby food and bodycare, they can get nappies in. Supplements include Quest, FSC, Viridian, Solgar, Kordels. Aromatherapy. Weleda homeopathy. A. Vogel tinctures. Ecover.

Harpenden

Graffiti
Omni Italian restaurant & pizzeria

32 Station Rd, Harpenden, AL5 4SE.
Open: Tue-Sun 12.00-14.00, 18-22.00 (last orders); Mon closed
Tel: 01582 460 300
www.graffiti-harpenden.co.uk

Italian restaurant with quite a few vegetarian starters, such as foccacia with olive oil, salt and rosemary £3.95, minestrone soup £5.95, lots of pizza and pasta £7-9, such as aubergine, olive chilli and garlic fiilling. Fixed price lunch £5.95 with house coffee. Soft drinks £1.95. Italian beer £3.10. Licensed.

Pizza Express, Harpenden

Omnivorous pizza restaurant

The Gate House, Harpenden AL5 2SN
Tel: 01582-765 714
Open: Sun-Thu 11.30-23.00,
Fri-Sat 11.30-23.30. www.pizzaexpress.com

In the centre of Harpenden. Glass fronted with view of the village green and next to the park. For menu see Bedford. Al fresco dining. Baby changing facilities.

Hatfield

Bella Italia, Hatfield

Omnivorous Italian restaurant

The Galleria, Comet Way, Hatfield AL10 0XY
Tel: 01707-251990
Open: Mon-Sun 10.00-22.30
www.bellaitalia.co.uk

Huge restaurant with lots of veggie options and they have a list of all the dishes suitable for vegans if you ask. Lunch from £5.95, 2 course evening set meal from £8.95. The pizza bases are vegan, so is the bruschetta starter and there are a couple of vegan pasta dishes. Step-free access, accessible toilets, braille and large print menu.

Hemel Hempstead

Tiki Cafe

Organic Fairtrade cafe

208 Marlowes, Hemel Hempstead, HP1 1BH
Tel: 01442-240108
Open: Mon-Sat 08.00-19.00, Sun 9-18.00
www.tikicafe.co.uk

We included this place because they have vegan chocolate cake! It's £2.70. Also vegetarian sandwiches and panini £3.40 which include falafel or vegetarian sausage. Filter coffee £1.90 latte £2.25, soya milk available. Smoothies £2.95. Bottled juices £1.40. Outside tables. Kids' play house. Kids' smoothies £1.50. No alcohol.

Woody's

Vegetarian cafe

19 Dickinson Quay, by the Grand Union Canal at Dickinson's Wharf, Apsley, near Hemel Hempstead HP3 9WG
Tel: 01442-266280
Open: Mon-Sat 10.00-22.00,
Sun 10.00-18.00
Train: Apsley (opposite)
Directions: On A4251 between Hemel centre magic roundabout and M25 junction 20.
www.woodyscafe.co.uk

In a beautiful, tranquil location alongside the Grand Union canal. English cuisine with Italian Influences. Lots of organic, Fairtrade, local, seasonal, gluten-free, vegan, no microwaves.
Soups with home-baked bread £5.50, or £3.75 as a starter. Stone-baked pizzas with vegan bases £5.95-9.50. Salads small £3.50, large £6. Filled pancakes, vegan options, £4.50-£7. Cookies, brownies, cakes and desserts £1.20-3.50 including vegan chocolate fudge cake, and vegan ice-cream is on the way.
Smoothies £3. Soft drinks £1.30. Pot of tea for one £1.50, large pot for 3 people £3.50, pot of herbal tea £1.85. Coffee £1.40, cappuccino and latte £1.75-1.95, hot choc £2. Filtered water 20p per glass, tap water free. Organic wines and beers, house wine £3.40 glass, £11 bottle.
Children welcome, 2 high chairs, colouring books and games. Outside seating, dog water (but only guide dogs inside). Disabled access. You can park at the back Mon-Fri 10-5pm, at other times there is the Papermill pub on the other side of the canal and offices where you can park out of hours.

Hemel Hempstead
Pizza Express, Hemel
Omnivorous pizza chain

5a Riverside, Hemel Hempstead HP1 1BT
Tel: 01442-256131
Open: every day 11.30-23.00
www.pizzaexpress.co.uk (menus)

They can make vegan pizzas if you ask them to leave off the cheese. Vegetarian options include margharita £5.75, giardiniera £7.95, and Veneziana £6.35. For menu see Bedford.

Hertford
The Good Food Shop
Health food shop

4 Old Cross, Hertford SG14 1RB
Tel: 01992-550101
Treatments: 01992-589439
Open: Mon-Sat 9.00-17.30, Sun closed
www.naturaltherapycentre.co.uk

Fridge and freezer with Redwood stuff, Swedish Glace, Booja Booja and B'Nice rice-cream, and they can get in whatever you need. Lots of local products such as hand-made soaps. Around 3000 product lines, half foods (and half of that organic) and half supplements and body care. Sandwiches and snacks for local office workers at lunchtime. Gluten-free, dairy-free, macrobiotic. Lots of sports supplements plus Solgar, Bioforce, Viridian, Nature's Answer, Quest, Health Sense. Aromatherapy products. Bodycare includes Green People, Jason, Dr Hauschka, Tisserand, Faith In Nature, Organic Surge. Baby bodycare. Homeopathy.
Hertford Natural Therapy Centre above shop offers over 20 qualified, registered complementary therapies practitioners. Gift vouchers available.
The manager tells us that most restaurants in Hertford have a vegetarian option, and **Lussmans** at 42 High Street SG14 1BY (Tel 01992-505329, www.lussmanns.com, also in St Albans and Bishop's Stortford) can cater for vegans and intolerances though there are no vegan dishes on the main menu.

Heydon
King William IV
Omnivorous country pub & restaurant

Chishill Road, Heydon, Cambridgeshire SG8 (technically in Cambridgeshire, for practical purposes it's Royston, Hertfordshire)
Directions: on the main road through Heydon, 17 miles from Cambridge off A505
Tel: 01763-838 773
Open: 12.00-14.30, 18.30-23.00, Fri-Sat 23.30, Sun 19.00-23.00
Lunch:12-14.00 (14.15 Sun)
Dinner: Mon-Thu 18.30-21.30, Fri-Sat 18.30-22.00, Sun from 19.00-21.00
www.kingwilliv.freeuk.com

16th century big Olde Worlde pub with some hanging oak tables in the bar area, a dining area, and a snug. There are some quiet alcoves for a business lunch or something more romantic. Vegetarian section on the menu with 7 dishes, and lots of vegetarian starters, changes with the seasons, and they get lots of vegans.
Starters such as soup £5.25, roasted peppers stuffed with spiced couscous £6.95.
7 main dishes, 3 with vegan option, £12.95-14.95, such as mushrooms in ale, risotto, enchiladas, ravioli, nut curry, shepherd's pie, 3-bean chilli with crispy corn tortilla and wild rice. Desserts £6-7 and vegans can have a fruit salad.
Lunchtime Mon-Sat 12.00-14.00 there's same menu plus panini, ciabatta and baguettes £6.95-7.50 such as roasted veg, jacket spuds £5.95.
House wine £3.85 glass, £13.95 bottle. Best to book, certainly Fri-Sat night and Sun lunch.. Well behaved children and dogs very welcome, 3 high chairs. 10

tables outside in the beer garden. Big car park. MC, Visa

Hitchin

Four Leaf Clover

Omnivorous cafe

2 Sun Street, Hitchin SG5 1AE
Tel: 01462-421878
Open: every day 08.00-20.00, Sun from 9.00

Turkish run cafe with British and European food. Vegetarian dishes marked on menu, not so much for vegans but they can make special things for you. This is the place to come in Hitchin for an all day full cooked veggie breakfast, £4.20 till 11.30, £5.50 rest of the day. Pizza £5.30. Baked potato and beans £3.50. Kids meal £3.20. Coffee £1.65-2.25, tea £1.35. Soft dinks and juices £1.30-2.20. Wine £2.70-3.60 glass, £12 bottle. Beer £2.85 for a pint or bottle. In summer they expand out onto tables in the square and have a food stall called Cafe Air.

Pizza Express, Hitchin

Omnivorous Italian restaurant

19 Market Place, Hitchin SG5 1DT
Tel: 01462-450 596
Open: Mon-Sat 11.30-23.00,
Sun 11.30-22.30
www.pizzaexpress.com

For menu see Bedford. Live jazz Tuesdays. Baby changing facilities.

Sun Spice

Omnivorous Indian restaurant

25 Sun Street, Hitchin SG5 1AH
Tel: 01462-421460
Open: Sun-Thu 18-23.00, Fri-Sat 18-24.00

Veg dishes £2.95-3.95. Set meal for 1 £12.95. Licensed.

Pizza Express in on the corner of Sun Street and the Market Place. Four Leaf Clover and Sun Spice are opposite, and further down the street are two Italian restaurants **Zizzi** and **Strada**. Off another corner of the square is the Greek restaurant **Bar Meze** with some veggie starters £3.95-4.95 such as falafel or roast aubergine, at 35 Bucklersbury SG5 1BG. Tel 01462-455566. Open Mon 18.30-22.00, Tue-Sat 12.00-14.00, 18.30-22.00. Licensed.
Between the centre and the station is **Sukawatee** Thai restaurant with a good vegetarian menu with lots of tofu. 80 Hermitage Rd, Hitchin SG5 1DB, tel: 01462-423733. Open: Tue-Sun 12-14.00, 18-23.00, Fri-Sat till 23.30, Mon closed. **Spice Shuttle** (end of Herts chapter) deliver curries to your door.

Health Emporium

Health food shop

16a High Street, Hitchin SG5 1AT
Tel: 01462-436 881
Open Mon-Sat 9.00-17.30, Sun 12.00-16.00
www.health-emporium.co.uk

Fridge with vegan cheeses and meat substitutes. Specialist in raw food, raw chocolate, Naked Trek, Bounce, carob bars. Freezer with burgers, Swedish Glace etc.
Lots of bodycare including Lavera makeup, Jason, Akin, and women's personal care. Kinder babycare. Vegan condoms. Ecover and refills.
Supplements include Solgar, Viridian, Nature's Aid, Nature's Plus, Lanes, sports nutrition including Nutrisport vegan pea protein. Homeopathy, remedies, aromatherapy. Homeopath and nutritionist in store most days, nails/beauty upstairs, food allergy testing once a month, hypnotherapist. Books on health and juicing. MC, Visa. Mail order.

Hitchin – continued

Farley's Hair Salon
Vegetarian hairdresser

68 Hermitage Road, Hitchin SG5 1DB
Tel: 07920-424426
Open: Tue-Sat 9.00-18.00, Thu till 22.00
www.myspace.com/farleyshairsalon

Now in expanded premises in the town centre on the road that leads to Windmill Hill park and the station. Relaxed salon using vegan organic products (one is vegetarian) and selling Giovanni vegan organic hair care products. Boys £20, girls £30. Colouring and highlights. Student discount £5. Fairtrade teas and coffees.

Kings Langley

Clare James
Health food shop

13a Hampstead Rd, Kings Langley WD4 8BJ (on main road A4251 near post office)
Tel: 01923-263195
Open: Mon-Tue, Fri-Sat 9.00-17.30, Thu till 19.00, Wed till 13.00, Sun closed

Lots of organic food. Chilled and frozen include Booja Booja, Swedish Glace and B'Nice rice-cream; Scheese, Vegerella and Redwood non-dairy cheese; seitan, tofu, soya mince. Bodycare. Supplements.

Letchworth Garden City

Fairhaven Wholefoods
Vegetarian health food shop

27 Jubilee Trade Centre, Letchworth Garden City, SG6 1SP. Tel: 01462-675300
Open: Mon-Sat 9.00-17.00, Sun closed
www.fairhaven.co.uk

Mostly vegan shop with organic fruit and veg, chilled and frozen including Redwood, Bute Island Sheese, Taifun. Lots of gluten-free and dairy-free products. Bodycare including Dead Sea Magik, Faith In Nature, Earth Friendly, Suma, Weleda, Organic Botanics, Eco Cosmetics, Lavera, Tiger balm. BioD, Ecover and refills, and Faith In Nature (Clearspring) cleaning products, supplements, homeopathy, aromatherapy. Baby bodycare. Women's personal care. Health and vegetarian cookbooks (Suma and Orangeburst).

Deliveries to Letchworth, Baldock and Hitchin, and occasionally beyond, ring for details.

Fairhaven Wholefoods suggest **L'Artista** Italian restaurant (9 Eastcheap, tel. 01462-689014) for veggie food, and there are several Chinese and Indian restaurants that have veggie dishes. **Spice Shuttle** (see end of Herts chapter) deliver curries to your home or business.

Potters Bar

Potters Bar Health Foods
Health food shop

21 The Broadway, Darkes Lane, Potters Bar EN6 2HX. Tel: 01707-652255
Open: Mon-Fri 9.30-17.30, Sat 9.00-17.00, Sun closed

Chiller with Redwood, Sheese, tofu, soya yogurt, Frys/Beanies, Swedish Glace, sweet (but not savoury) takeaways including date or apricot slice.

Lots of bodycare including Faith In Nature, Aloe Vera, Organic Surge, Green People. Supplements including Lifeplan, Crest, Solgar, Nature's Own, Vogel. Women's personal care. Ecover cleaning products. Homeopathy, aromatherapy. A few books. Therapy room with massage, homeopathy, reflexology, Reiki, Bowen, Craniosacral etc.

Radlett

Pizza Express, Radlett

Omnivorous Italian restaurant

114 Watling Street, Radlett WD7 7AB
Tel: 01923-859 111
Open: every day 23.30-24.00
www.pizzaexpress.com

Large rear garden and front terrace seating. Outside dining. Baby changing. For menu see Bedford.

Rickmansworth

Zaza

Omnivorous Italian restaurant

21 Church Street, Rickmansworth WD3 1DE
Tel: 01923 772287
Mon-Fri 12.00-14.30, 18.00-22.30; Sat 12.00-22.30; Sun 12.00-14.30, 17-22.00
www.zazarestaurant.co.uk

Sister restaurant to Sazio in St Albans in a 1682 building. Plenty of veggie options. Pasta £6.40-8.90, risotto primavera £9.90, pizza £6.50-7.90. Wine from £12 bottle, large glass £4. Private dining room for up to 30. Eat in the garden in summer.

Sawbridgeworth

Full Of Beans

Health food shop

2 Church Street, Sawbridgeworth CM21 9AB
Tel: 01279-726002
Open: Mon & Sat 10.30-16.30,
Tue-Fri till 9.30-17.15, Sat till 16.30, Sun closed

Orgnanic fruit and veg. Fridge and freezer. Swedish Glace vegan ice-cream, B'Nice to order. Redwood fake cheese and meats. Baby body products. Bodycare including Herbatint and Naturetint. Supplements Solgar, Quest, Vogel, Nature'sPlus, Udo's. Ecover refills. Aromatherapy, Bach flower remedies, homeopathy.

St Albans

Nimatt's Bar Meze

Omnivorous Cypriot tapas bar

8 Adelaide Street, St Albans AL3 5BH
Open: Mon 18.30-23.30 (closed lunchtime); Tue-Sat 12.00-14.30 & 18.30-23.30;
Sun 12.00-15.00 & 19.0-22.00.
Tel: 01727-847799
www.barmeze.co.uk

There are no starters or mains, you order a snack or a main meal simply by varying the number of dishes chosen. Veggie dishes £3.65-5.95, all served with hot pitta, include houmous, roasted aubergine and tomato, roasted red pepper, green beans in tomato and herb sauce, broad beans, mixed veg, charcoal grilled mushrooms, falafel, rice with onions and peppers. Chips £2.95, olives £1.50. Children welcome, high chairs. Wine £3.75-4.25 glass, from £12.95 bottle. Bottled beers £3. Ouzo £1.50, spirits £2.50. Soft drinks £1.80. Tea and coffee from £1.50. MC, Visa.

Pizza Express, St Albans

Omnivorous pizza chain

11/13 Verulam Road (A5183), St Albans AL3 4DA. Tel: 01727-853 020
Open: Sun-Tue 11.30-22.30,
Wed-Sat 11.30-23.00
www.pizzaexpress.co.uk

For menu see Bedford.

Sazio

Omnivorous Italian restaurant

5a High Street, St Albans AL3 4ED
Tel: 01727-812 683
Open: Mon-Fri 12-15.00, 18.00-22.30; Sat 12-23.00; Sun 12.00-22.00
www.sazio.co.uk

Lots of veggie options. Vegetarian pizza £5.95 lunch, a la carte £8.90, bases and garlic bread are vegan, and where

St Albans – continued

Wagamama, St Albans

Omnivorous Japanese restaurant

Unit 6, Christopher Place, St Albans AL3 5DQ
Tel: 01727-865 122
www.wagamama.com
Open: Mon–Sat 12.00–23.00 Sun –22.00

See Manchester entry for menu. Disabled friendly.

Zizzi

Omnivorous Italian restaurant

26 High Street, St Albans AL3 4EL
Tel: 01727-850 200
Open: Mon–Sun12–23.00 Thu–Sat 23.30
www.zizzi.co.uk

Owned by ASK chain. Pizza bases are vegan and can be made without cheese, from £7–10. If you are gluten-intolerant you can bring your own base and they will add toppings. Also salads and lots of pasta, and they can make something special for you. Wine from £12.95 bottle, £3.65–4.75 glass. Children welcome, high chairs, kids' menu £5.95. Outside seating in summer. MC, Visa.

B Healthy

Health food shop

41 The Quadrant, Marshalswick, St.Albans AL4 9RB. Tel: 01727-831112
Open: Mon–Sat 9.30–17.00, Sun closed
www.b-healthy-home.co.uk

Fridge with vegan cheeses, tofu, meat substitutes. No freezer. Gluten-free foods. Plamil, Montezuma, Divine and

possible will adapt dishes to make them vegan. House wine £12 bottle, £4 glass, £3 small. Children welcome, high chairs and special menu. (Previously called The Pasta Bowl)

sometimes Organica vegan chocolate. Bodycare from Jason, Weleda, Green People, Faith In Nature, Natracare. Weleda and Green Pepole organic Babies, nappies.
Supplements include Solgar, Lifeplan, Viridian, sports nutrition. Homeopathy and remedies. Therapy room with food sensitivity testing, osteopathy, Indian head and holistic massage, reflexology, Reiki, EST emotional freedom technique.

Stevenage

Pizza Express, Stevenage

Omnivorous Italian restaurant

124-126 High Street, Stevenage SG1 3DW
Tel: 01438-361270
Open: Mon–Sat 11.30–23.00, Sun 11.30–22.30. www.pizzaexpress.com

In the heart of the old town. Outside dining. baby changing. For menu see Bedford.

Tring

The Green House

Vegetarian restaurant

50 High Street, Tring HP23 5AG
Tel: 01442-823993
Train: Tring station
Open: Mon–Sun 12.00–23.00,
kitchen closes 21.30 (Sun 20.30)
www.thegreenhousetring.co.uk (menus)

New vegetarian international wholefood restaurant in a grade 2 listed 16th century building, fitted out in a contemporary style. Organic where possible, with plenty for vegans, they cook with coconut oil and even make their own vegan cashewnut ice-cream.
Lunch: £5.95–£9.45 main course includes falafel with fruit couscous and sweet chilli sauce; or bean and chick pea burger in a bun with guacamole and salad.

Evenings starters £4.45-7.05 include black olive tapenade with raw pitta bread, or seasonal salad with omega-3 dressing and miso walnut pate. Dinner mains £8.95-11.95 include Thai marinated vegetable coconut curry with savoury sweet parcel and brown basmati rice.

Desserts offer plenty for vegans such as chef David's special raw apple pie, or rhubarb crumble with cashew kream, £5.95.

All alcohol is vegan organic. Wines include Chardonnay or Merlot £14.95 bottle, 250ml glass £5, 175ml £3.50. Samuel Smiths lager and bitter, Westons pear and apple cider £3.80.

High chairs, children's menu. Can cater for gluten-free and raw. Low energy lighting, toilets flushed with rainwater. They compost kitchen waste and grow many of their herbs and salad greens. Visa, MC.

Harmony

Health food shop

53 High Street, Tring HP23 5AG
Tel: 01442-822311
Open: Mon-Sat 9.00-17.30, Sun closed

Organic bread by Paul's Bakery delivered Thursdays. Chilled and frozen, tofu, Redwood fake cheese and meat, Fry's, frozen veg. Swedish Glace, Booja Booja and B'Nice rice-cream, lollies. Thai and Japanese foods. Montezuma, Divine and the full Plamil range of chocolate. Organic body and skincare. Organic baby food and toiletries. Supplements include Solgar, Viridian, Biocare, Creative Nature, Nature's Plusand herbs, spirulina. Organic Natural by Nature aromatherapy. The owner can recommend local complementary practitioners. Lots of health and recipe books, cards and candles. They can order special items.

Ware

The Lounge

Omnivorous pizza-pasta restaurant

7 Amwell End, Ware SG12 9HP
Tel: 01920-463358
Open: Mon 11.00-17.00, Tue-Sat 11.00-23.00, Sun closed. www.wareonline.co.uk

Previously Soul Mama's vegetarian restaurant, now a family-owned Italian restaurant that continues to cater for veggies and can make things vegan too. Light lunch menu with 5 veggie pizzas £5.50-£7, can leave off cheese for vegans and bases are vegan, or create your own from the toppings list. Several pastas £5.80-£7. Ciabatta £3.70-4.70 with fillings including falafel, hummous, grilled veg. Salads £5.50-£7. House wine £13 bottle, £3.50 glass. Cappuccino/latte £1.90, soya milk. Children welcome, high chairs. MC, Visa.

Watford

ASK Restaurant

Omnivorous pizza & pasta restaurant

The Former Post Office, Market Street, Watford WD18 0LG. Tel: 01923-213 111
Open: Sun-Thu 12-23.00, Fri-Sat 12-23.30
www.askrestaurants.com

Pizza bases are vegan, can be without cheese, £7.75. House wine £12.65 bottle, £3.55-4.65 glass. Children welcome, high chairs. MC, Visa.

Cafe Mezza

Omnivorous Lebanese restaurant

144 Lower High Street, Watford WD17 2EN
Tel: 01923-211 500
Open: every day 12-23.00
www.cafemezza.com

Lots of veggie and vegan meze dishes £3.40-4.70, including falafel,

EAST Hertfordshire

hummous, babaganoush, tabouleh, fatoush salah with croutons, kibbe potatoes, spring Vegetable skewer or casserole £7.95. Two hot pitta-style take-away sandwiches £3.80: Al Bustan with charcoal grilled vegetables and baba ganoush; and falafel. House wine £10.95 bottle, £3.50-4.95 glass. Children welcome, high chairs. Sometimes belly dancing Fri-Sat 8pm. MC, Visa.

Pizza Express, Watford

Omnivorous pizza restaurant

137 High Street, Watford WD17 2ER
Tel: 01923-213 991
Open: Mon-Sun 11.30-24.00

In a 1614 building next to the Harlequin Centre in the centre of town. Vegan no problem. Baby changing facilities. Meeting room.

Ambala Foods, Watford

Indian sweet shop

96 Queens Avenue, Watford WD18 7NS
Tel: 01923-817 560
Open: every day 11.30-23.00
www.ambalafoods.com

Plenty of sweets and savouries for vegetarians, only samosas for vegans.

Panacea Health

Health food shop

The Harlequin Shopping Centre, Unit 137, Upper Mall, Watford WD17 2UB
Tel: 01923-227297
Open: Mon-Sati 9.00-18.00, Thu till 21.00, Sun 11.00-17.00

The biggest of four stores that used to be called Victoria Health. Specialist breads such as rye and gluten-free. Fridges and freezers with sprouts, tofu,

vegan cheeses and meat substitutes such as Fry's, Goodlife, RealEat, Swedish Glace, Booja Booja, B'Nice, ready meals. Organic tinned foods. Vegan chocolate by Plamil and Organica, lots of snacky things.
Bodycare by Green People, Jason, Akin, Aubrey, Lavera, Saaf, Weleda, Natracare, Organic Children, Earth Friendly Baby. Supplements by Solgar, Viridian, Biocare, Lamberts, Nature's Aid, sports nutrition. Nelson, Weleda and Bioforce Homeopathy, Bach flower, Pukka herbs. Sometimes food allergy testing. Alma Win vegan laundry products, Ecover, Earth Friendly. MC, Visa.

Welwyn Garden City

Pizza Express, Welwyn

Omnivorous Italian restaurant

40 Howardsgate, Welwyn Garden City AL8 6BJ
Tel: 01707-334 231
Open: Tue-Sat 11.30-22.30, Sun-Mon 11.30-22.00. www.pizzaexpress.com

For menu see Bedford. Baby changing.

Natural Health, Welwyn

Health food shop

36 Wigmores North, Welwyn Garden City AL8 6PH. Tel: 01707-392020
Open: Mon-Sat 9.00-17.30, Sun closed
www.naturaltherapycentre.co.uk

Fridge and freezer with Redwood stuff, Swedish Glace, Booja Booja and B'Nice rice-cream, and they can get in whatever you need. Lots of local products such as hand-made soaps.
Around 4,500 product lines, half foods (and half of that organic) and half supplements and body care. Gluten-free, dairy-free, macrobiotic. Lots of sports supplements plus Solgar, Bioforce, Viridian, Nature's Answer, Quest, Health Sense. Aromatherapy products. Bodycare includes Green

People, Jason, Dr Hauschka, Tisserand, Faith In Nature, Organic Surge. Baby bodyare. Homeopathy.
Natural Therapy Centre behind shop offers 15 qualified, registered complementary therapies practitioners. Gift vouchers available. the owner of the Good Food Shop in Hertford (see above for details of product lines). Also a therapy centre with 15 practitioners for consultation and treatments six days a week. Mail order from the website.

Local Group
N Herts Vegetarians & Vegans

www.nhvegetariansandvegans.org.uk
www.myspace.com/nhv

Networking, socialising and campaigning.

Curry home delivery
Spice Shuttle, Letchworth
Omnivorous Indian caterer

S & S Catering Services Ltd, Unit 20 Green Lane, Letchworth SG6 1HP
Open: every day 12.00-24.00
Tel: 0800 862 0666
www.spiceshuttle.co.uk

Curry delivery service 6-7 miles around Letchworth including Hitchin, Baldock and nearby villages. Enter your postcode on the website to see if they deliver there. A green V shows vegan items on the vegetarian menu, with separate woks and freezers for veg food. Starters around £2. A dozen main dishes £4.50-£5, or £2.70 as a side dish, in mild, normal, hot or extra hot, such as dhansak, karahi, daal, aubergine with potato. Rice, brown rice, naan, chapati, paratha, £1.30-2.20. Pickles, chutneys and salads. Minimum order £8, cash or credit card. They aim to deliver within 45 minutes. Order from the website for 5% discount or by phone. 5% discount if you order 2 hours in advance, and 10% off first order, for a maximum 20% discount. Can supply pubs for a curry night, free delivery over £50 within 30 minutes.

Hertfordshire chain stores
Holland & Barrett
Health food shop

115 High St, **Barnet** EN5 5UZ
Tel: 0208-449 5654

12a South St, **Bishops Stortford** CM23 3AT
Tel: 01279-651 637

Unit 187c The Marlowes Centre,
Hemel Hempstead HP1 1BB
Tel: 01442-211 356
Open: Mon-Sat 9.00-17.30, Sun 11-17.00

25/27 Birchley Green, **Hertford** SG14 1BN
Tel: 01992-504 751

99 Hermitage Road, **Hitchin** SG5 1DG
Tel: 01462-451 643

11 Leys Avenue, **Letchworth** SG6 3EA
Tel: 01462-678289

6 Angel Pavement, **Royston** SG8 9AS
Tel: 01763-249 468

61 St Peters St, **St Albans** AL1 3EA
Tel: 01727-845 333
Open; Mon-Sat 9.00-17.30, Sun 11-17.00
(Wed, Sat market days from 08.00)
Chiller with pastries, freezer.

Unit 44 Queensway, **Stevenage** SG1 1EE
Tel: 01438-727 749

Unit 73 The Pavillion, High Street, **Waltham Cross** EN8 7BZ. Tel: 01992-652182

105 High Street, **Watford** WD17 2DQ
Tel: 01923-221 602
Open: Mon-Sat 9.00-17.30, Sun 11-17.00

54 Howards Gate, **Welwyn Garden City**
AL8 6BP. Tel: 01707-376 285

Tourist information:
www.enjoyhertfordshire.com
www.touristnetuk.com/SE/herts

Leicestershire

Leicester is a great place for vegetarians to live and visit if they like curry, as it has a huge range of veggie eateries, possibly due to the large populations of Hindus, Jains and students who live here.

Leicester city centre has a lot of character, with more small shops than chain stores, and lots of lovely old buildings, though it certainly isn't quaint. It is a small city, yet has good facilities, including a huge library, friendly pubs and possibly the largest outdoor market in Britain, where you can buy very cheap fruit and veg, textiles and clothes. There are several large parks on the edges of the city centre, and you can walk by the canal which runs from north to south through the middle of the city.

There is a strong green movement in Leicester, and cycling paths are better than average, though air pollution can be a big problem in hot weather. The city also seems to have a strong spiritual feel. There is an annual vegan festival around October.

49	Ashby de la Zouch	www.visitleicester.co.uk
49	**LEICESTER hotspot**	www.goleicestershire.com
54	Loughborough	www.leicesterveganfair.co.uk
55	Market Harborough	
55	Chain stores	
55	Local group	
55	Leicester Vegan Fair	

Indigo Indian vegetarian restaurant, Leicester

Ashby de la Zouch
Jane's Health Foods
Health food shop

7 Rushtons Yard, Ashby de la Zouch LE65 1AL. Tel: 01530-416741
Open: Mon-Sat 9.00-17.00, Wed 9-15.00
www.janeshealthfoods.co.uk
www.lifebalancing.co.uk

Organic, fair trade, gluten free and dairy free products. Fridge with dairy-free cheeses and meat replacers but no freezer. Bodycare includes Faith In Nature, Jason, Weleda, Natracare. Babycare including Weleda, Earth Friendly Baby, Jason. Supplements and sport nutrition. Essential oils. Ecover and refills. Health and diet books and relaxation CD's.
Treatments include Bowen technique, food intolerance testing, homeopathy, Reiki, holistic, sports and Indian head massage, stress management and relaxation.

Leicester vegetarian restaurants
Ambica Sweetmart
Vegetarian Gujarati Indian restaurant

147 Belgrave Road, Leicester, LE4 6AS (opposite Law Street). Tel: 0116-266 2451
Open: Mon-Fri 11.30-20.00,
Sat-Sun 11.30-21.00
www.ambicas.co.uk

Sweet shop downstairs, and a family-run restaurant reopened upstairs in June 2009. Thali is their speciality. Eat well for around £10-15 for 2 people with food from all over India. Over 20 starters, 12 curries, Karai (Balti) specials, south Indian dishes like dhosa and uttapam. Regular £4.99 or special thali £6.99. Children very welcome, 2 high chairs. MC, Visa. Outside catering for 50 to 3,000.

Bobby's
Vegetarian Indian restaurant

154 Belgrave Road, Leicester LE4 5AT
Tel: 0116-266 0106
Open: every day 11-22.00
www.eatatbobbys.com

Indian vegetarian restaurant on Leicester' "curry mile" with some vegan curries, chapattis and snacks. Specialise in Gujarati food. Thali £6.49. All day buffet every day £6.99, £3.99 children. House wine £2.50 glass, £7.95 bottle. High chairs. Function room, outside catering.

Chaat House
Vegetarian Indian restaurant

108 Belgrave Road, Leicester LE4 5AT
Tel: 0116-2660 513
Open: Wed-Mon 12.00-20.30, closed Tue

There is no such thing as bad Indian food in Leicester which has curry houses everywhere. However there is such a thing as outstanding Indian food which you'll find here being munched by the local vegetarian Buddhists, Hindus, Sikhs and vegan Jains. Specialise in north Indian, but also have south Indian food. Thali £7.50-8.50. No alcohol. Children welcome, high chairs. Visa, MC. Outside catering.

Good Earth Restaurant
Vegetarian restaurant

19 Free Lane, Leicester LE1 1JY
Tel: 0116-262 6260
Open: Mon-Fri 10.00-15.00, Sat 10-16.00
good.earth-restaurant@virgin.net

Buffet-style daytime restaurant which always has something vegan. Salads £3.25-4.25. Hot main dishes £4.25-6.25 such as beany casserole with roasted veg. Home-made cakes and

EAST Leicestershire

slices, crumbles such as lemon syllabub, strawberry eton, including vegan, 80p-£2.20. Freshly squeezed orange juice and and home-made lemonade £1.10. Beer or glass of wine £2.20. Children welcome, high chair. No credit cards.
They have a gourmet evening once in a while. Downstairs they have an aromatherapy shop with a wide range of potpourris and essential oils.

Leicester vegetarian restaurants

Indigo

Vegetarian Indo-Chinese restaurant

Indigo at the Fosseway, 432 Melton Road Leicester LE4 7SN. Tel: 0116-261 1000
Open: Mon-Fri 12.00-15.00, 18.00-23.00; Sat-Sun 12.00-23.00 (last orders 22.30) (last orders half an hour before closing); www.indigos.co.uk (menus)
See picture page 48 and front cover.

Popular Indo-Chinese vegetarian restaurant with a fairly extensive menu of South Indian and Indo-Chinese dishes £4.50-£6. Freshly made pizza £4.50-£10, vegans can have without cheese. Indian style pasta £6. Mon-Fri lunch buffet 12.00-14.30 £6.99.
Set menu for 15+ people (50% deposit when booking) £10 (children 5-8 £6.50), for choice of 2 starters and 4 mains, add £2.50 (£1) for another starter and fizzy drink, £15 (£8.50) for 3 starters, 5 mains and dessert, of which carrot halva is vegan.
Freshly squeezed juices £2-3, soft drinks and water £1.20, hot drinks £1.50-£2. House wine £10 bottle, £2.75-3.50 glass. Lots of draught and bottled beers £2.95. Spirits £2.25. Children welcome, high chairs. MC, Visa, Amex. Outside catering with on site-cooking, they do lots of summe garden parties.

Mirch Masala

2 vegetarian Indian restaurants

Unit 19-20 Belgrave Commercial Centre, Belgrave Road, Leicester LE4 5AV.
Tel: 0116-261 0888
Open: every day 11.00-22.30

37-39 Market Street, Leicester LE1 6DN
Tel: 0116-247 0080
Open: Mon-Thu 09.00-21.00, Fri-Sat 09.00-22.00, Sun 11.15-17.00
www.mirch-masala.co.uk

Family oriented Indian vegetarian restaurants with Mexican, Italian, Indo-Chinese and South Indian menus. Same menu in both.
South Indian starters £2.50-£3.50, such as spiced crushed lentil balls covered in deep fried pastry, and crispy puri filled with potatoes and chickpeas.
Main dishes include masala dosa, £3.75-5.75; idli sambhar - flat rice and lentil flour cakes served with coconut chutney and sambhar (lentil soup); and mixed vegetable curry. Wraps £4.50-495 with fillings ranging from herb and garlic to Mexican rice or chilli.
House wine £2.25, bottle £8.99. Fresh juice bar with smoothies. High chairs. MC, Visa, Amex.

Sardaar

Vegetarian Indian restaurant

30 Narborough Road, Leicester LE4 5AT
Tel: 0116-299 3300
Open: Mon-Sun 10.00-22.00, last orders 21.30, last take-out 21.45
www.sardaar-restaurant.co.uk

North Indian Punjabi on the south-west side of town. Great value dishes £2.90-3.99, 70% vegan. Samosas 30p. Thali £4.90. Desserts include non-dairy gulab jamun, 2 for £1.20. Hot and cold drinks 80p-£1.20. No alcohol. Children welcome, high chairs. Toilets not disabled accessible (upstairs). Free delivery up to 2 miles over £20. No credit cards. Student discount 10%. Oustide catering.

Sayonara Thali

Vegetarian Indian restaurant

49 Belgrave Road, Leicester LE4 6AR
Tel: 0116-266 5888
Open: Mon-Sun 12.00-21.30, Sat till 22.00

North, South and Gujarati dishes, thalis and take-away. Choice of 50 starters £2-£4.95, curries £4.75, thalis £6.75-7.75, always vegan options, but not for dessert. Beer £2.50 bottle, house wine £2 glass, from £7.90. Children welcome, high chairs. Visa, MC.

Shankar Paubhaji

North Indian vegetarian restaurant

21 Melton Road, Leicester LE4 6BN
Tel: 0116-2669 522
Open: every day 11.00-22.00

Thali £3 with two curries, rice, chappati. Curries all under £3.50, rice £1.50. Samosas £3.25. One Chinese dish, Hakka noodles with veg £2.50.
Also take-away. 20 seats, take-away, free delivery under 5 miles, £10 minimum. No alcohol. No credit cards, maybe in future.

Sharmilee Restaurant

Vegetarian Indian restaurant & shop

71-73 Belgrave Road, Leicester LE4 6AS
Restaurant: 0116-261 0503
Mithai Shop: 0116-266 8471
Open: Tue-Fri 12-14.30, 18.00-21.30, Sat-Sun 12.-21.30, Mon closed unless bank holiday or special occasion such as Diwali
Shop: Tue-Sun 9.30-21.00 (Sat till 21.30)
www.sharmilee.co.uk (menu)

Family restaurant established for 30 years with North, South, Gujarati and Indo-Chinese. Average £10 for a meal. Thali £6.95, special thali £8.95, the dessert can be fruit salad for vegans, but you could ask them to get something suitable from the sweet shop downstairs. House wine £2.50 glass, £6.95-12.95 bottle. Children welcome, high chairs. MC, Visa. Outside catering. Air conditioned.
Shop does sweets and savouries such as samosas, and they can get take-aways from the restaurant upstairs.

Shivalli

Vegetarian South Indian restaurant

21 Welford Road, Leicester LE2 7AD
Tel: 0116-255 0137
Mon-Fri 12.00-15.00, 18.00-23.00
Sat 12.00-23.00, Sun 12.00-22.00
www.shivallirestaurant.com

New south Indian Karnataka restaurant opened by the old chef and manager from the old Halli vegetarian restaurant on Granby Street. Wood panelled walls and floor and modern wooden tables, discreet lighting and a chandelier. Local vegans report plenty of vegan options.
Mon-Fri 12.00-15.00 3-course buffet eat as much as you want lunch (not bank holidays), £4.95 for starter, main and dessert. Buffet includes popadoms, starters with chutneys several main dishes and a dessert, they can make a vegan one if you ask when you arrive. Lunch box £2.95 with curry of the day and rice.
Over 50 a la carte menu items. Unusual starters £2.50-3.75 include rassam or tovve soups, upma (semolina with nuts, green chillies and ginger), vade lentil doughnuts, ambade potato and nut balls in gram flour. Dosas and uttappam £3.49-5.25. Curries, sides and salad £3.75-4.25. Rice and exotic rice with all sorts of extras such as cashews, tamarind, lentils, coconut,

£1.75-3.75. Indian breads £1.45-1.65. 3-course thalis £9.95.
Desserts £1.99-3.45, they have vegan versions of jaggerry dosa pancake and kesari bhath semolina with raisins and cashews.
House wine £2.50-3.50 glass, £9.99 bottle. Freshly made juices £2.45, normal juice £1.60. Coffee from £1.50, Indian coffee £1.95, ask in advance and they'll get some soya milk.
Children most welcome, high chair. Take-away 10% discount. Groups of 25+ can have a buffet dinner served. NCP Newark Street car park nearby or York Road behind the restaurant, or nearby streets. Catering inside and out.

Leicester omnivorous
Bo Bo Oriental
Omnivorous Chinese/Thai take-away

61 Leicester Rd, Oadby, Leicester LE2 4DF
Tel: 0116-271 2324
Open: Mon-Sun 17.00-23.30, Fri-Sat 24.00
www.boboriental.com

Popular with local vegans. with at least a dozen veggie dishes £2.50-4.50 including mixed veg with beancurd or cashews, veg crispy duck, sweet & sour, curry. Rice from £1.60, chips £1.40. Banana or pineapple fritters £1.80. £1.30 delivery charge, free over £20 within 3 miles. Visa, MC 30p extra.

Oriental Chinese
Omnivorous Chinese restaurant

70 High Street, Leicester LE1 5YP
Tel: 0116-2532 448
Open: every day 12.00-23.30
www.orientalchinesebuffet.co.uk

Lots of vegetarian dishes such as stir-fried veg, crispy veg with chili and garlic, monk's veg and bean curd, around £5. £4.80 buffet before 4pm, evening £6.99, Fri-Sat evening £7.99. House wine £10 a bottle, £3.15 glass. Children welcome, 2 high chairs. MC, Visa.

Leicester shops
Currant Affairs
Vegetarian wholefood shop

9A Loseby Lane,, Leicester LE1 5DR
Tel 0116-251 0887
Open: Mon-Sat 9.00-17.30, Sun closed

Organic, natural and Fairtrade foods. Lots of savoury food and cakes, the majority made on the premises. Take-away pastries for around £1, including several filled rolls, pies, pasties, vegan and vegetarian pizza. Most of the cakes are vegan, flapjacks, vegan cheesecake all 99p. Plamil, Montezuma, Divine, Booja Booja vegan chocolates. Vegan "cheese", Redwoods sausages, bacon, etc. Swedish Glace. Vegan frozen meals. Local organic bread suitable for vegans, lots of gluten-free. They will order stuff in for you.
Bodycare include Faith In Nature. Women's personal care. Ecover cleaning products. They don't sell supplements. 10% discount for Vegetarian or Vegan Society members.

Green & Pleasant Wholefoods
Omnivorous wholefoods and health foods shop

59a Queens Road, Leicester LE2 1TT
Tel: 0116-270 2974
Open: Mon-Sat 9.15-17.30, Sun closed

Veggie boxes. Organic and veg on the way. Local organic bread. Fridge and freezer with tofu, pies, meat substitutes, non-dairy cheese, Swedish Glace, frozen ready meals such as butternut squash roast, spicy beanburgers, sutaki pies, veggie haggis, Tuscan bake,

Moroccan pie and casserole, aduki cobbler, organic veg tofu pie.
Bodycare including Weleda, Faith In Nature, beautiful local organic soaps. Natracare women's things and Mooncup. Baby and pregnancy, nappies, foams and lotions.
Ecover and BioD cleaning products.
Supplements include Lamberts. Remedies include Weleda, New Era and Bach flower. They do changing window displays with something going on instore such as homeopathy week or Father's Day. They can recommend local practitioners.

Leicester Wholefood Co-op

Organic omnivorous co-operative

Unit 3, Freehold Street, off Dysart Way, Leicester LE1 2LX (east of the centre)
Tel: 0116-251 2525
Open: Mon-Thu 9.30-18.00, Fri 9.30-19.00, Sat 9.30-17.00, Sun closed
www.wholefoodcoop.co.uk (3000 products online)

Warehouse-style organic and health-food shop. Specialists in organic, vegetarian, vegan, dairy-free, gluten-free, fairly traded, and locally produced food. All vegan items are labelled as such on the shelves. Over 70 kinds of bread and rolls. Fridges with soya milk and yogurt, and deli items such as hummous, olives, etc. Frozen section with veggie burgers, sausages, Cheatin turkey roast, fishless fishcakes, Swedish Glace, Tofutti, B'Nice rice-cream. Herbs and spices. Bodycare includes Faith In Nature, Green People, Pitrok, Toms, Urtekram. Natracare. Baby care. Essential oils. BioD, Clearspring, Ecover cleaning products. A few books. Deliveries.

Wellbeing

Health food shop

1-3 Odeon Arcade, Market Place, **central Leicester** LE1 5HJ. Tel: 0116-253 9097
Open: Mon-Fri 9.00-17.30, Sat 8.30-17.00, Sun closed

35 Bell Street, **Wigston,** south Leicester LE18 1AD. Tel: 0116-281 1233
Open: Mon-Fri 9.00-17.30, Sat 8.30-17.00, Sun closed

Fridge and freezer with vegan cheeses, meat substitutes, Swedish Glace. The central branch has lunchy things like wraps and veggie samosas.
Bodycare includes Jason, Dr Hauschka, Faith In Nature, Avalon, Weleda, Dead Sea Magik, Natracare. Baby bodycare.
Ecover, BioD and the new Method cleaning products. Homebrew kits.
Wide range of supplements including Solgar, Vogel, VIridian, Nature's Aid, Lifeplan, Quest, Udo's oil, sports supplements. Bach remedies, Weleda homeopathy, essential oils. Sometimes a nutritionist in store for the day. Complementary therapies rooms being added to both shops. 10% discount to vegetarians and vegans.

GNC

Health food shop

18 Silver Street, Leicester LE1 5ET
Tel: 0116-262 4859
Mon- Sat 9.00-17.30, .Sun 11.00-17.00

This shop used to sell lots of take-away food, but now it's most supplements and sports nutrition.

Loughborough
Salims
Omnivorous Indian restaurant

9 Leicester Rd, Loughborough LE11 2AE (High Street End). Tel: 01509-213200
Open: Mon-Sun 18.00-24.00, Fri-Sat 00.30
www.salims.co.uk

Starters including various soups £2.50-2.75. 6 o7 main dishes such as curries £4.75-5.75 and about 10 side dishes. Thali £8.90. House wine from £9.90 bottle, £2.50 glass. Free delivery over £12 within 5 miles, or £1 charge.

The Thai House
Omnivorous Thai restaurant

5a High Street, Loughborough LE11 2PY
Tel: 01509-260030 no incoming calls
Open:
www.thaihouseloughborough.co.uk

Main dishes £5.95-6.50 such as cashew or crispy bean curd with Thai veg. Rice £1.95, coconut rice £2.95. Note they have a fish tank.

Mr Chan's
Omnivorous Chinese restaurant

14 Bedford Square, Loughborough LE11 2TP
Tel: 01509-216216
Take-away: 01509-218880
Open: Mon-Sun 12.00-14.30, 17.30-23.00, Fri-Sat till 23.30

Veg and bean curd dishes £3.70. Rice £1.80-2.50. Chips £1.50. Banana or

The Green House, first and second Thu-Fri evenings of the month

apple fritter £2. Set meal £9 each for minimum 2 people. All day buffet Sunday £10. Licensed.

Market Harborough
The Green House

Vegetarian restaurant

Joules Yard, rear of 53-55 High Street, Market Harborough LE16 7AF (go down alley between Joules Clothing at 53 and Grangers Estate Agents at 55)
Tel: 01858-463250
Open: First two Thu and Fri pairs of every month 18.00-20.30 (last orders)
www.joulesyard.co.uk
enquiries@joulesyard.co.uk
See picture left and front cover

Partners Kerry the chef and Nathan with help from mum Ann run a vegetarian restaurant here the first two Thursday and Fridays of the month in premises borrowed from the licensed cafe Joules Eating House, which does not normally open Thu-Fri eve. They have their own utensils that are never used for anything non-veg, whilst other equipment is thoroughly cleaned before. Separate fridge and freezer. Menu changes with the seasons.

Starters around £4 such as potato wedges with mixed beans and salsa. Mains around £7 such as Thai chicken-style curry, veg casserole and dumplings, bbq hotpot. Fabulous vegan desserts around £4 such as chocolate and brandy torte, lemony treacle tart, coconut rice pudding, ice-cream. Fairtrade vegetarian and vegan drinks, wine £2.25 glass, bottles from £9, organic beer from £2.60 bottle, and coffee £1.20. MC, Visa.

See website for sample menu. Good for kids, high chair. Groups of 16 or more can book the entire restaurant with a tailored menu. 25 seats inside and more outside in fine weather. Advance booking by phone or email is preferred though not essential.

Health food chains
Holland & Barrett

Health food shop

48 Castle Street, **Hinckley** LE10 1DB
Tel: 01455-251258

5-6 Humberston Mall, Haymarket Centre **Leicester** LE1 3YB. Tel: 0116-251 6270

33 The Horsefair Street, **Leicester** LE1 3BP
Tel: 0116-262 1547

9 Market Place, **Loughborough** LE11 3EA
Tel: 01509 269159

11 Manor Walk, **Market Harborough** LE16 9BX. Tel: 01858-431 250

Julian Graves

Health food shop

3 Clock Tower Mall, **Leicester** LE1 3YA
Tel: 0116-253 1115

7 Cheapside, **Melton Mowbray** LE13 0TP
Tel: 01664-482848

Local Group
Leicestershire Vegetarian/Vegan Group

www.leicesterveggies.org.uk

Meets first Thursday of the month 7.30pm at the Friends Meeting House, Queen's Road, Leicester. Membership gets you discount at many local shops and restaurants. Monthly meals out.

Leicester Vegan Fair

www.leicesterveganfair.co.uk

Annual autumn vegan fair, the perfect way to spend Saturday in Leicester.

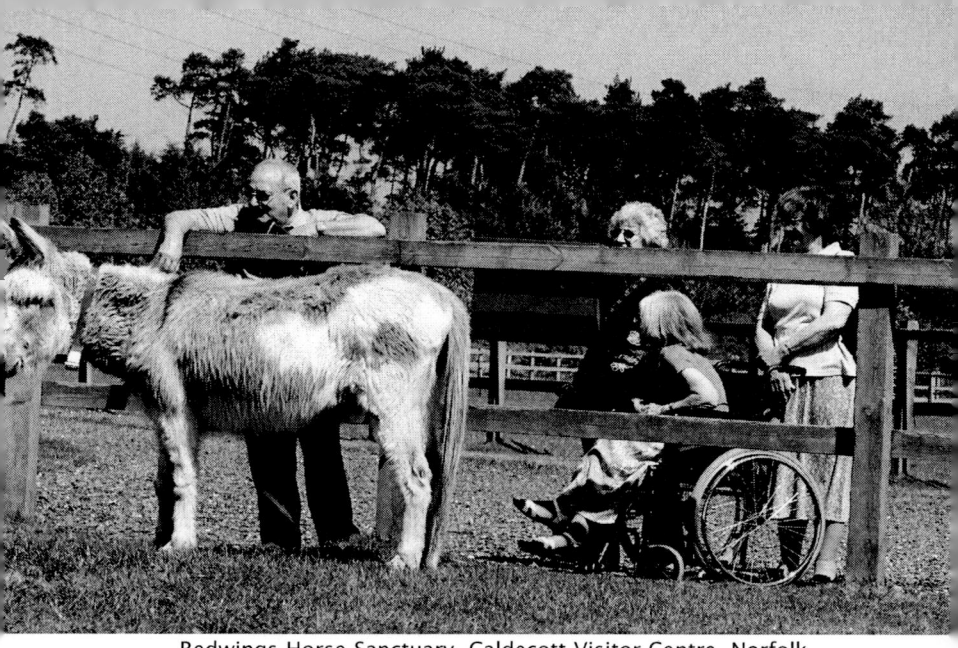

Redwings Horse Sanctuary, Caldecott Visitor Centre, Norfolk

West Lodge vegetarian guest house, Drayton, Norwich

Norfolk is a mostly flat county with huge fields and a very open skyline. The area attracts many birdwatchers, partly due to its beautiful, clean beaches. The North Norfolk coast is renowned for its coastal bird population; from little terns on Blakeney point in early summer to large flocks of migratory geese in early autumn. The seals on Blakeney point are a must see, boat trips run throughout the year. The coastline is dotted with delightful villages with something to offer in both winter and summer.

The only large city is **Norwich**, which has lots of ancient, historic winding streets and a suprisingly bustling, cosmopolitan feel. Culturally Norwich is a rich and diverse city with its thriving theatres and art scene, the Theatre Royal, Maddermarket Theatre, Puppet Theatre, Playhouse and Norwich Arts Centre. There is also outside theatre in the parks during summer months where you're encouraged to take a blanket and a picnic, or the multi-screen cinema complexes for that rainy day. Norwich is in the top 10 places to shop in Britain with malls, independent designer shops and colourful market stalls. There are two vegetarian guest houses, **West Lodge** and **Number 15**. **The Greenhouse** and **Pulse Cafe** are the main vegetarian eateries, plus **Amity Point** and the **Tea House** veggie cafes, and **Vegeland** and **Butlers** take-aways. Lots of other places offer veggie food, including two cafes in arts centres, **Frank's Bar** and some fabulous wholefood stores.

There are several golf courses and the N1 national cycle route is on the doorstep. The quality of the light throughout the year is much sought after by both wildlife and landscape artists and there are some excellent galleries. Outside Norwich eat at **Les Amandines** vegetarian restaurant in Diss and a couple of great country pubs **The Brick Kilns** and **The Green Man**.

Information provided by West Lodge vegetarian guesthouse

www.visitnorfolk.co.uk
www.visitnorwich.co.uk
www.norwich12.co.uk
www.maddermarket.co.uk
www.norwichplayhouse.org.uk
www.puppettheatre.co.uk
www.theatreroyalnorwich.co.uk
www.norfolkbroads.com

Accommodation	58
Animal sanctuaries	61
Attleborough	62
Dereham, Diss, Fakenham	63
Harleston, Holt, Little Plumstead	64
Little Snoring	65
NORWICH veggie hotspot	65
Sheringham	72
Swaffham, Walsham, Wymondham, Chain stores, Local group	73

Norfolk

West Lodge

Large Victorian house set in a mature enclosed garden. Newly landscaped subtropical garden with meditation and smoking decks. Set behind electric gates for added privacy and security. Small conference facilities, holistic weekend breaks and retreats including life coaching, garden design and feng shui astrology. There is a very private yet light airy and contemporary feel to West-Lodge, which makes it ideal for business or pleasure. Built in 1890 it retains much of its original charm and character.

Price per room: 1 kingsize double with 5-piece bathroom £95; 2 doubles ensuite £75; wing with 1 double/twin, 1 twin and shared bathroom £125 the lot, ideal for family or group of friends. Single person £20 off double room price. Room 3 has a sofabed for a third person £25 extra.

Breakfast includes fruit juice, cereals, seasonal fruit, white or wholemeal bread, preserves. Cooked options mostly contain egg or cheese but also mushrooms, grilled peppered tomatoes, beans, saute sweet peppers, filled pancake, bagels. Vegan margarine, muesli, soya milk and yoghurt available. Food is organic, Fairtrade and locally sourced where possible. Most dietary requirements can be catered for. Breakfast in room if ordered evening before.

At the moment evening meals are only available with prior arrangement and cost an average of £25 per head for 3 courses accompanied by a glass of wine. Evening trays £5-6.50 such as home-made soup with bread and fruit plus a pot of tea or coffee or a mug of hot chocolate.

Rooms have tv, dvd player, wifi, hot and cold refreshments. Ironing facilities, hairdryer. Books, games and dvd's available.

Norwich

Vegetarian Guesthouse

24 Fakenham Rd
Drayton
Norwich
Norfolk NR8 6PR
(NW side of Norwich)

Tel: 01603-861191

www.vegetarian-bedandbreakfast-norwich.co.uk
info@vegetarian-bedandbreakfast-norwich.co.uk

Train station: Norwich 4 miles, bus or taxi

Open: all year

Directions: 100 miles north-east of London. Good rail links and dual carriageway or motorway almost all the way. From A11 or A47 clockwise around the outer ring road, turn left onto the A1067 Fakenham road. Drayton is about 3 miles from this point.
Stansted (1.5 hours drive) and Norwich airport (5 minutes).

Parking: available

Children welcome in some rooms, no special facilities

No smoking inside. Smoking deck outside.

No pets (they have cats)

10% discount for Viva! members

See photo page 56

Greenbanks Hotel

Hotel and restaurant with vegetarian proprietors in the heart of the Norfolk countryside. There are nine luxury ensuite rooms consisting of doubles and twins for £44-56 per person, and family rooms and large suites for £99-160 per room bed & breakfast. Single occupancy £65-75.

Begin your day with cereal and juice followed by a cooked breakfast of herbed potato pancakes, beans, spiced tomatoes, home made veggie sausages and muffins or nut scones. Soya milk, soya yoghurt and vegan margarine are available. Veggie and vegan specialities are available on request.

A three course dinner is offered in their licensed Alexanders restaurant for £23. It could be miniature vegetable spring rolls followed by ginger roasted root vegetables with stuffed peppers and for dessert, apple cake and coconut custard. 50% of the produce is organic. Open to non-residents. Vegan, coeliac, diabetic and all diets catered for.

Greenbanks is set in eight acres of meadows and has a bog garden, wild flower walk and lakes. Indoor heated swimming pool for all guests use with a sauna and jacuzzi to relax in, late evening or early morning.

The coast and beaches are nearby as well as Peddars Way walk and Thetford Forest where you can walk or cycle.

Not far away is the thriving city of Norwich with its huge churches, interesting castle and museums. It has the best night life in the region behind Cambridge.

Tea and coffee making facilities and televisions are in the rooms.

Wendling

Omnivorous hotel & restaurant

Swaffham Road
Wendling
Norfolk NR19 2AB
England

Tel: 01362-687 742

www.greenbankshotel.co.uk

Email: jenny@greenbankshotel.co.uk

Train station: Norwich, 20 miles, then bus

Open: all year

Directions: Midway between Swaffham and East Dereham on A47, turn off at sign saying Wendling/Longham

Parking: 20 spaces

Children are welcome and they have facilities such as high chairs.
Cots £8 per night

Pets by arrangement £5

Disabled access: 5 ground floor rooms and full access to showers

Credit cards accepted

No smoking throughout

Please state that you are veggie on arrival or when booking

Accommodation, Castle Acre
Old Red Lion
Wholefood vegetarian bed and breakfast / hostel

Bailey Street, Castle Acre, PE32 2AG
Tel: 01760-755 557
Train Station: Downham Market, 12 miles
Bus route: National Express from Victoria to Swaffam daily
www.oldredlion.org.uk
oldredlion@yahoo.co.uk

Two doubles (one ensuite), two twins, one dorm room and one family room £25-£35 per person per night. Dorms from £17.50 bed & breakfast. Discretionary rates negotiable for longer stays and groups, who can book the entire centre. +20% single occupany or one-night stay. Evening meal by arrangement. You can use the kitchen to cook your own meals. Dogs and children by arrangement. No smoking throughout. Yoga classes, days and events. Art workshops, see www.chalkies.tsites.co.uk

Accommodation - Norwich
Number 15
Vegetarian bed & breakfast

15 Grange Road, Norwich, Norfolk NR2 3HN
Tel: 01603-250283 (9.00-20.00 best)
Open: all year
www.number15bedandbreakfast.co.uk
Email: ianry2@hotmail.com

In a quiet, tree-lined road with parking, near veggie cafes. 2 large double rooms £23.50-30 per person depending on room and number of nights. Single £40, 2-5 nights £35, 6+ £32. Minimum 2 nights at weekends. Feather/down free bedding. Lounge with tv, cd's and board games. Totally non-smoking. No children or pets. Complementary therapies available. Cash or cheque with card, no credit cards.

Accommodation West Runton
Hollyhock House
Vegetarian bed & breakfast

Church Close, West Runton, Norfolk NR27 9QY.
Tel: 01263-837325, Mobile 07815 597145
Open: all year
Train: West Runton, 10 minutes walk or they can collect (45 minutes to Norwich)
www.hollyhockhouse.info
hollyhockrunton@tiscali.co.uk

Detached family home overlooking the sea, offering a comfortable, tranquil space in which to relax and unwind and, should you require them, a variety of holistic therapies to enhance your stay. Rooms at the back have sea views.
One double ensuite, two twins with shared bathroom, £30 per person, or £35 as single. Minimum 2 nights or £5 supplement.
Reflexology, Indian head massage and aromatherapy available. Bird watching, beach access with swimming or sunbathing, fossil hunting. Unique geology, wild flowers, country walks.
Eating places, village shops and golf nearby. The local pub has veggie food and the Pepperpot restaurant in the village is good for veggie and vegan food. It's a 15 minute walk to the health food shop in Sheringham (page 72). Coasthopper bus.
Children welcome, high chair, bring your own cot. Parking on drive. No smoking in the house. No pets - Chloe the Lurcher might not approve, kennels nearby. Cash or cheque only.

Hillside Cottages
Self-catering cottages

at the Hillside Shire Horse Sanctuary, West Runton NR27 9QH (on the north Norfolk coast between Sheringham & Cromer)
Tel: 01603-736200
Open: all year round
www.hillside.org.uk/help-accomm.htm
contact@hillside.org.uk

Two self-catering cottages in the Shire Horse sanctuary, one sleeping 8 for between £365 and £725 per week, ideal for 2 families, and one sleeping 2 for between £225 and £395 p.w. When the sanctuary is closed they will give you a tour of it.

Animal Sanctuaries
Hillside Shire Horse Sanctuary & Vegan Cafe
Horse & animal sanctuary with vegan cafe and two self-catering cottages

At **West Runton** NR27 9QH. (20 miles from the original Hillside Animal Sanctuary)
Tel: 01603 736200 for latest Open Day info or see website www.hillside.org.uk/OpenDaysatWestRunton.htm
Open April–Nov (check website exact dates)
Apr-May open Sun-Thu (closed Fri-Sat);
Jun-Aug open Sun-Fri (closed Sat);
Sep-Oct open Sun-Thu (closed Fri-Sat).
Opening times 10.00–17.00
Also open Easter weekend Fri-Mon
Directions: Follow the brown signs "Shire Horse Sanctuary" off A149 Cromer to Sheringham Road

Not just horses, also donkeys, cows, sheep, pigs, hens, alpacas, rabbits. Admission adults £5.95, senior citizens £4.95, U-16 £3.95, U-3 free. Disabled access. Dogs welcome on lead. Car park. Shop.
Vegan cafe with cakes, sandwiches, light snacks.

Hillside Animal Sanctuary
Animal sanctuary

Hill Top Farm, Hall Lane, **Frettenham**, near Norwich NR12 7RW
Tel: 01603-736200 for latest Open Day info or see website www.hillside.org.uk
Open one Sunday per month in summer 13.00–17.00, check website for when, do not just turn up.
Directions: Take B1150 North Walsham Road from Norwich outer ring road. Follow 3 miles to White Horse Pub in Crostwick on your right. Take next left into Hall Lane, then first left.
www.hillside.org.uk

Hillside Animal Sanctuary was founded in 1995 to help and campaign for animals in need and most importantly, to bring public awareness to the millions of animals suffering every day in the intensive factory farming industry. Hillside has given sanctuary to 300 horses, ponies and donkeys, but most residents have been rescued from the farming industry. Meet 900 animals and birds including cows, pigs, sheep, horses, ponies, donkeys and many others. Gift and bric-a-brac shops. You can adopt an animal (makes a great present) from £10 and receive a photo and a report twice a year.

Hillside has two sanctuaries The original one at Frettenham, near Norwich, is home to 900 rescued animals and birds and is open to the public one Sunday afternoon per month in the summer. The newly acquired shire horse sanctuary, which has other animals too, is 20 miles away by the sea at West Runton, and is open most days in the summer, with a vegan cafe and self-catering holiday cottages.

Redwings has two horse sanctuaries in Norfolk (next page, open summer) and Essex (page 25, open all year).

Animal Sanctuaries

Redwings Horse Sanctuary Caldecott Visitor Centre
Animal sanctuary with cafe

At Caldecott Hall, situated on the A143 between Great Yarmouth (2 miles) and Beccles NR31 9EY (opposite Fritton Lake Countryworld at Caldecott Hall)
Tel: 01508-481000
Open: Easter or start of April to end October every day 10.00-17.00. Entry is free.
www.redwings.org.uk

The original sanctuary of 3 open to the public, the other two are in Essex and Warwickshire, and they have others for more nervous animals. This one near Great Yarmouth has over seventy acres of paddocks and is home to rescued horses, ponies, donkeys and mules, including handsome shire horses, tiny Shetlands and mischievous donkeys. There are tractor rides (weather permitting), walking tours, horse care demos and a children's play area as well as the chance to rub noses with the residents. The site also has a café, gift shop, information centre, charity shop, tombola and the Horse Wise Education Centre with horsey facts and interactive displays.

Omnivorous café has jacket potatoes, paninis and baguettes, soups, cakes, afternoon tea, Fairtrade teas and coffees. Wednesday 10% discount for senior citizens.

The stable yard and first paddocks are fully accessible to wheelchairs. Wheelchair for loan, fully accessible WC. In the picnic area some of the tables are wheelchair friendly. Disabled toilets. Dogs wecome on lead. Birthday parties. Caldecott Hall golf course nearby. Garden centre down the road.
Other centres in Essex (page 25, open all year) and Warwickshire.

Attleborough

Oasis World Peace Cafe
Vegetarian cafe

Amoghasiddhi Buddhist Centre, Cyprus House, Queens Square, Attleborough, Norfolk NR17 2AE.
Tel: 01953-451 937
Open: Tue-Sat 9.00-15.30, Mon-Sun closed
www.amoghasiddhi.org.uk/Visit_us.htm

Busy cafe with a peaceful atmosphere, run by volunteers, 15 miles west of Norwich on the way to Thetford. Part of a network of Kadampa tradition (Mahayana Buddhism), with centres and World Peace cafes opening up around the UK and the world.

All day cooked breakfast £4 with sausages, hash browns, mushrooms, baked beans, bread. Light lunches include jacket potatoes £3.65 with two fillings and salad; large bowl of soup with bread £4; panini £3.95 made to order with a salad; cup of soup & sandwich combo £3.50; spicy wedges with salsa and salad £4; nachos and spicy beans with dip £3.50. The menu is expanding.

Homemade cakes are very good value at £1.30-1.70, chocolate cake is vegan. Full range of coffees from £1.65. Mug of tea £1. Soya milk available. Juices and soft drinks 80p-£1.

Very child-friendly, there is a lounge off the main cafe where they can roam with baby chair and kids' books. Garden with seating in spring/summer, dogs welcome. Cash or cheque only.

Drop in meditation classes here and in Norwich, Bury St Edmunds. Gorleston and Wyondham, and Buddhist study programmes and retreats, see website for details. Book shop. Drop in meditation Wed 12 till 1 during term times, £4.50. Lounge can be rented for groups and courses, with food to order. Opportunities to volunteer and get work experience with free meditation.

Dereham
Guy's Health Store
Health food shop

35 Norwich Street, Dereham NR19 1AD
Tel: 01362-693402
Open: Mon-Sat 9.00-17.00,
Wed till 13.00, Sun closed

Lots of packaged organic foods. Bodycare is mainly Faith In Nature. Lots of Weleda homeopathy and remedies, essential oils. Supplements especially Quest, Lifeplan. Ecover cleaning. No credit cards.

Diss
Les Amandines
Vegetarian restaurant

Norfolk House Yard, St Nicholas Street, Diss IP22 4LB. Tel: 01379-640 449
Open Tue-Sat 10.00-16.00, Sun-Mon closed

Vegetarian and vegan café-restaurant established 1987, in the centre of the town, a stone's throw from the old church and market place. They serve breakfasts, teas, cakes and lunches.
Always have a vegan soup £3.95 with local bread. Main meals £6.95 can be chilli with jacket potato or basmati rice and salad £6.95, Creole pate and beetroot hummous with toast and olives and salad £6.95, lemon and spinach chickpea tagine with couscous. Sandiwiches and panini made to order £4.50-£5.
Gluten-free and vegan cake available £2.20. Coffee £1.50, cappuccino £1.90, Pot of tea £1.40-1.60. Wine £2.95 small glass, £5 large, £14.95 bottle. Bottled beer and organic cider £2.95.
Open twice a month for special **musical Saturday nights** with live jazz, blues, flamenco or folk, booking essential. 3-course set meal £25 with choice of 4 starters, 4 mains, 8 desserts.

Natural Food Store
Vegetarian health food shop

Norfolk House Yard, St Nicholas Street, Diss IP22 4LB. Tel: 01379-651 832
Open: Mon-Fri 9-17..30 (Tue, Sat 17.00), Sun closed

Adjacent to Les Amandines. They sell organic bread, local organic pasties, their own cakes (some vegan), savouries, deli stuff like wrapped vine leaves, and vegan cheeses. Freezer with Booja Booja and Swedish Glace, meat substitutes. The chiller has homemade hummous, pate, etc.
Boycare includes Weleda, Essential Care (local organic company), Faith In Nature and their own skincare range, Natracare. Weleda and Organic Babies. Ecover and Clearspring cleaning.
Supplements include Nature's Own, A Vogel, Weleda homeopathy. Lots of essential oils and bases. Permaculture and Resurgence magazines.

Fakenham
The Larder
Health food shop

10 Norwich Street., Fakenham NR21 9AE
Tel: 01328-855306
Open: Mon-Sat 9.00-17.00, Sun closed

Fridge with vegan cheeses, tofu, sausages etc. Freezer with meat substitutes, Swedish Glace. Plamil vegan chocolate.
Bodycare includes Faith in Nature, Green People, Suma, Weleda, Natracare. Baby things. Supplements include Power, Nature's Aid, Quest, Lifeplan, Lanes. Homeopathy, flower remedies, essential oils. Free magazines. No credit cards.

Harleston

Town Living
Crafts and wholefoods shop

Town Living incorporating Host of Hats
4 London Road, Harleston IP20 9BW
Tel: 01379-853258
Open: Mon-Fri 9.00-17.00, Thu till 13.00, Sat 9.00-15.30, Sun closed

---

Harleston is a nice little town with a lot of independent shops, Budgen and a Coop, 3 proper greengrocers and a Wednesday market 7am till 2pm. But don't come Thursday afternoon when everyone is closed. Town Living is a crafts, hats for hire, sewing and knitting shop with several rooms and at the back of the store lots of wholefoods from Rainbow in Norwich.
Local organic bread. Fridge with tofu, vegan cheese, sausages. Bodycare includes Faith In Nature, Weleda, Bentley Organics, Avalon, Natracare, and baby stuff from Avalon and Faith,
Supplements by Nature's Own and Cotswold Health, Helios remedies and Tisserand aromatherapy. Ecover and refills. Craft books and magazines. They run craft workshops. MC, Visa.

Holt

Nature's Haven
Health food shop

35 Bull Street, Holt, Norfolk NR25 6HP
Tel: 01263-478355
Open: Mon-Sat 9.00-17.00, Sun closed

No fridge or freezer. Gluten and wheat-free. Plamil and Montezuma vegan chocolate. Bodycare includes Dr Hauschka, Skincare, Avalalon, Organic Surge, Green People, Organic Surge, Barefoot Botanicals, Natracare. Maltex nappies.
Ecover, BioD, Clearspring, Method and some Suma household products. Supplements include Nature's Own, Bio Health, Biocare, FSC, Quest, Higher Nature, Nature's Aid. Weleda and Helios homeopathy, Healing Herbs flower essences, essential oils. MC, Visa.
Holt is a lovely little Georgian market town 6 miles from Hollyhocks guest house. Byfords bistro has veggie food.

Little Plumstead

The Brick Kilns
Omnivorous pub, restaurant & B&B

Norwich Rd, Little Plumstead, Norwich NR135JH (on B1140 Acle road 4 miles east of Norwich ring road, regular bus)
Tel: 01603-720 043
Open: 7 days 11.00-23.30
Food 7 days 12.-00-14.00, 18.00-21.30 (last orders). See photo front cover (the pink one)
www.thebrickkilns.co.uk (menu)

Proper English country pub, built over 400 years ago, with oak beams and real fires in winter, with a restaurant serving hundreds of vegetarian meals per week. 30 items on the vegetarian menu with vegan items marked, and a cook who only makes the veggie Food cooked to order so no problem to make things vegan or gluten-free, separate chip pan. 17 veggie main courses £7.95-8.95 are served with either vegetables or chips and peas/mushy peas, or a side salad or rice. Vegetarian gravy can be ordered before receiving your meal. Vegan mains on the regular menu include spicy chick peas with onions, peppers and tomato; nut goulash; Red Dragon casserole with aduki beans; chilli bean casserole; ratatouille. Also specials such as soya shepherd's pie in the winter.
Desserts £4.50 include a vegan cake, and they have soya cream and 3 flavours of Swedish Glace vegan ice-cream.
House wines £2.25 small glass, £4.25 large, £6 carafe, £8.95 bottle. Fine wines £15-16. Real ales.

Well behaved kids welcome, but not if they're noisy or run around. Baby changing. Terrace with a few tables, covered smoking area. Wheelchair toilet and access throughout. Dogs welcome outside but not inside except guide dogs. Wifi. MC, Visa.

From 2010 they offer **accommodation** in 3 en-suite bedrooms, providing an ideal base from which to visit the nearby Norfolk Broads.

The conservatory has far-reaching views across fields with sheep, goats, horses and donkeys, and is available for private dining, meetings, weddings and wakes (not Fri-Sat evenings and Sunday lunch).

Little Snoring
The Green Man
Omnivorous pub-restaurant

Holt Road, Little Snoring, Fakenham NR21 0AY (on the main road)
Tel. 01328-878350
Pub : Mon-Fri 12.00-14.00, 17.00-23.00; Sat-Sun 12.00-23.00
Food Mon-Fri 12.00-14.00, 17.00-21.00; Sat-Sun 12.00-21.00
Website on the way

Fantastic, a big country family pub with Nepalese chefs. Like the previous owners until 2009, the new ones are offering veggie/vegan and gluten-free dishes. Food cooked to order. Main dishes £7.25-7.95 include potato and spinach, kabuli channa chickpeas dal, maknhi black lentils, curries. Basmati rice £2.35, Kashmiri £3.35. Naan breads.

Wine from £12.50 bottle, £3.40 small glass, £4.60 large. 3 real ales. Coffee.

Children welcome, high chairs, booster seat, kids menu has pasta or they can rustle something up. Massive garden with seating. Dogs welcome in bar but not restaurant. Big car park. 5 caravan pitches outside, no hookups. MC, Visa.

NORWICH - veggie hotspot
Amity Point Cafe
Vegetarian and raw cafe

16 Onley St, Norwich NR2 2EB (corner Durham Street). Tel: 01603-699 907
Open: Wed-Sun 10.00-17.00, Mon-Tue closed
www.amitypoint.co.uk
www.thegoldentriangle.co.uk

New corner cafe in Norwich's Golden Triangle, the studenty, young professional area between the centre and University of East Anglia. They only buy from small suppliers and use only Fairtrade, that's not "whenever possible", that's always. If you like spending an afternoon at Pogo Cafe in London then you'll love this. They don't do hot meals, just sandwiches, juices, hot drinks, raw cakes, and soup in the cooler months.

Sandwiches, made to order with wholemeal bread from a nearby bakery, £2.75-3.25, such as hummous, avocado and sun-dried tomato. Toast £1.95.

They are raw treat specialists: vegan cheesecake £1.50, choc brownie £1.35, energy balls and almond halva £1.10.

Freshly squeezed juices £1.60-2.40, such as apple, carrot and ginger; Mean Green £2 with rocket, celery, green apple, ginger, lemon and cucumber. Spiced warmed juice £1.90-2.20. Pots of tea £1.60, mug £1.30. (Soya) latte, chai latte, cappuccino, mocha £1.60-2.20. coffee £1.40-1.70.

Some outside tables. They have kids' books, games, a couple of toys. Dogs welcome. Secondhand books for sale 75p-£2. Cash only.

EAST
Norfolk

NORWICH - vegetarian
Butlers
Vegetarian take-away & bakery

98 Vauxhall Street, Norwich NR2 2SD
Tel: 01603-665 066
Open: Mon-Fri 08.30-14.00, Sat-Sun closed
www.butlersofnorwich.co.uk

Take-away main meals only (no seats), £2.35 per portion such as pasta or lentil and aubergine bake, changes daily. Salads by weight, around 80p per 100 grammes portion. Slab cakes £3.50, some vegan, gluten or sugar-free. Bottled and canned drinks. Bread from their bakery.
Vegetarian food suppliers to caterers, catering for weddings and functions, specialise in vegan and gluten-free.

The Greenhouse Cafe
Vegetarian cafe, take-away & shop

in Norwich's Environment Centre, 42-46 Bethel St, Norwich, NR2 1NR
Tel: 01603-631 007
Cafe: Tue-Sat 10.00-17.00, lunch 12.00-16.00; Sun-Mon closed
www.greenhousetrust.co.uk

Fairtrade, organic **cafe** serving home made range of light meals. Vegan gluten-free soup of the day with bread £3.85 eat in (£3.50 take-away). Daily special £6.95 such as pies, chilli, curries, vegan moussaka and lasagne, with veg or salad. Savoury dish with side salad £5.50 (£5). Ramekin of hummus with wholewheat pitta and big salad £5.50. Portion of hummus £1.30, olives £1.50, bread 70p. Seasonal vegan salad bowls £4/£4.50. Ploughmans salad with the option of vegan cheese £6.95.
Sandwiches £3.50 (£3 take-away) made to order with organic wholewheat or 100% rye bread. Home-made pasties and savoury rolls £2.25.

Cakes from £1.90 and savouries with vegan and gluten-free options. Teas and coffees 80p-£2.80, e.g. large pot £2.50. Hot or cold cordials £1. Organic vegan wine £3 glass, £10 bottle, local beers and ciders £2.50, though only with food.
Quiet well supervised children welcome, but not if they run around. Please turn off mobiles. The café is part of the Greenhouse Trust, a charity to promote sustainable living and there is plenty on the shelves to read.
The **shop** aims to provide a basic, organic wholefood diet with some extra treats such as organic wines, spirits, local beers and the local Booja Booja chocolate truffles. They have vegan cheeses, desserts and sausages. Range of organic flours, even spelt flour. Locally made Essential skin care products, greeting cards and exquisite Fairtrade (and better) gifts including crafts and Montezuma chocolates. Range of local organic apple juices. Green stationery and magazines. BioD clearning products. MC, Visa, 50p charge under £10.

Pulse Cafe
Vegetarian cafe & restaurant-bar

The Old Fire Station Stables, Labour In Vain Yard, Guildhall Hill, Norwich NR2 1JD (above Rainbow Wholefoods, off Guildhall St)
Tel: 01603-765562
Open: Mon 10.00-18.00, Rue-Wed 10.00-22.00, Thu-Sat 10.00-23.00, Sun 10.30-16.00
www.pulsecafebar.co.uk (menu)

Cafe by day, restaurant-bar by night, lots of vegan and gluten-free food. Very international menu plus daily specials, lots of organic. Courtyard for outside dining.
Cafe menu available 10.00-18.00: Wraps, panini and bruschetta include spicy Mexican beans with guacamole;

roasted Aubergine; smoked paprika laced hummous with roasted red pepper, black olives and roquette; all served with a mixed leaf salad for £5.25. Pulse club sandwich £4.95 is toasted wholemeal bread containing smoked tofu marinated in basil oil, iceberg lettuce, sliced beef tomato and vegan mayonnaise. Two slices of thick wholemeal toast £1.90. Side orders of olives, caper berries, roasted almonds, mixed leaf salad, ciabatta, rice cakes, oat cakes, hummous or guacamole with bread, all £2.10.

Restaurant menu available 11.00-22.00:

Smaller dishes: green pea & mint soup; Vietnamese style spring roll with sambal sauce; tofu, cinnamon & almond filo parcel on roquette; all served with organic wholemeal bread £4.50. Chickpea burger with onion ring, guacamole and roasted tomato £5.50. Lots of salads with bread £6.50 such as bulgur wheat with baby spinach & butternut squash; pasta with roast Mediterranean vegetables and pesto. Pizzas £6.95-7.50.

Larger dishes £7.50 with salad or bread, such as baked spicy bean enchilada; Northern African pastille or aromatic veg, pine nuts & apricots wrapped in filo pastry; Thai curry with coconut rice; Oriental stir-fry with lemon & coriander rice; Moroccan rice with wedges of butternut squash and harissa sauce.

Desserts £4.95 include fresh fruit skewers with vegan chocolate dip, champagne rhubarb trifle. Cakes £2.40, cookies and muffins £1.90, some gluten-free and vegan. Ice-cream including vegan £1.25 scoop, £3.25 3 scoops.

Organic wines £4.55 glass, £15.95 bottle, beers from £3.30 pint or bottle. Fruit juices £2.35, smoothies £2.50.

Children welcome, high chairs, baby changing. Visa, MC, Amex.

The Tea House
Vegetarian cafe

Wrights Court, 5 Elm Hill, Norwich NR3 1HQ
Tel: 01603-631888
Open: Mon-Sat 11.30-18.00, Sun closed

In a historic cobbled lane in the old part of town near the cathedral. Tables inside and out in the small garden at rear. Children welcome.

Chunky sandwiches made to order and light lunches around £3.50 such as soup with bread. Chilli £4.50 with tortilla and salad.

Cakes £2.50, only occasionally vegan, muffins, chocolate. Tea £1.20 pot, coffee £1.75 medium, £1.85 latte/cappuccino. Soft drinks £1.20, juices £1.85, mixed berry smoothie £2.50.

Vegeland
Vegan take-away

28 Cattle Market Street, Norwich NR1 3DY (City centre, opposite Castle Mall)
Tel: 07845-282127
Open: Mon-Fri 12.00-17.00, Sat-Sun and bank holidays closed
www.vegeland.co.uk

Mainly Chinese food, also salads, and frozen food to take home. Hot and cold buffet, £2.50 for a self-serve box, £3 large, £3.50 all-you-can-eat. Noodles, fried rice, Thai curry, sweet and sour veg, soya protein, stir-fry that changes every day such as broccoli and black beans, mini spring rolls, pasta and salads. Vegan hot dogs and burgers £2.50. Sandwiches from 2009. No seats, but you can stand at a table to eat.

Norwich - omnivorous

Assembly House Restaurant

Omnivorous restaurant & cafe-bar

The Assembly House, Theatre Street
Norwich NR2 1RQ (next to Theatre Royal)
Tel reception: 1603-626402
Restaurant: 01603-627526
Open: Mon-Sat 10.00-19.00; l
Sun 11.00-16.00
www.assemblyhousenorwich.co.uk

Proper restaurant, cafe-bar and patisserie in a grade 1 listed Georgian building that is part of Norwich 12, the UK's finest collection of individually outstanding heritage buildings spanning the Norman to modern eras. (see www.norwich12.co.uk) There is a good vegetarian selection and also wheat-free and vegan. It's very popular for afternoon tea. Often a pianist Sunday lunchtime and with afternoon teas. They use a lot of local veg and the bread baked in-house is also for sale.

Starters include soup £4.95 with their own bread; roasted red pepper salad with couscous. Light lunches such as sandwiches and baguettes £4.95, like hummous with a pot of ratatouille and black olives. Ever-changing menu of hot dishes, £6.95 as a light meal with salad and bread, or £9.95 as a larger portion with veg selection, such as pumpkin, sage and hazelnut risotto; red lentil and apple cakes with chilli cherry tomato ketchup; big salads. Big on desserts, vegans can have roasted pineapple with chilli and vanilla. Pre-theatre suppers 5-7pm, 2 courses for £13.95.

Morning coffee with homemade cakes from £2.25, including vegan carrot cake and shortbread. Fairtrade coffee and a big range of leaf teas. Coffee or pot of tea £1.95. Soya milk available.

House Wine £3.95 glass, £15.95 bottle. Local Woodfords bottled beer £2.95 pint.

Kids welcome, high chairs. Wifi. Beware leather sofas. Free art exhibitions. You can hire the place for weddings, proms, parties. Paying car park. MC, Visa. Other Norwich 12 buildings nearby include the castle, cathedral, and the Forum with the tourist information office and library.

Expresso

Omnivorous cafe

St Georges Street, Norwich NR3 1BA
Tel: 01603-768881
Open: Mon-Sat 07.00-17.30,
Sun 9.00-17.00
www.expresso-online.co.uk

Independent cafe using local ingredients and suppliers where possible. Homemade soups £3.95 with bread include minestrone, or spiced savoury apple with coriander oil, usually vegan. Grilled ciabatta or focaccia such as roast Mediterranean vegetables £3.50 takeaway, or eat in £5.50 with salad and dressing. Cakes but not vegan.

Italian Segafredo coffee for latte or cappuccino £2.15. Teas and herbal £1.30. Frappé iced drinks £2.50. They have soya milk. Lots of soft drinks £1-£1.44, Innocent smoothies £1.90, organic juices £1.95. Bottled beer £2.95. Wine £3.40 glass, £12.95 bottle. Children welcome, no high chair. Outside seating, dogs can sit with you at the front. MC, Visa,

Frank's Bar
Omnivorous cafe-bar

19 Bedford St, Norwich NR2 1AR (centre)
Tel: 01603-618 902
Bar open: Tue-Thu 10.30-24.00;
Fri-Sat doors close 02.00, stop serving 02.30;
Sun 10.30-23.30; Mon closed
Breakfast: Tue-Sat 10.30-12.00,
Sun 11-18.00
Food menu: Tue-Fri 12.00-15.00, 18.00-22.00; Sat 12.00-22.00.
www.franksbar.co.uk (menus)

Recommended to us by local veggies, the seasonally changing menu has some excellent and clearly marked veggie and gluten-free tapas-style nibblers and main courses, most vegan. The examples below an idea of the type of food available. Table service.
Tapas and nibbles: Spicy roast almonds £2. Frank's bar platter for 1 or more £3.50 with bread, olives, oils and hummus. Add £1.50 per extra person. Gluten-free vegan lemon cookies £1.40. Couscous with feta & broad beans £3. Marinated aubergine, pinenuts & herbs £3.50. Bruschetta with hummus, piquillo peppers & rocket £4. Falafels £4. Side salad £2.50. Mixed herb olives £2.50. Portion of mixed breads £1.50.
Meals: Hummus sandwich with sunblush tomato pesto, rocket & pinenuts £4.50. Middle Eastern mezze £6 with falafels, marinated aubergine, piquillo peppers, olives & dips. Italian antipasti salad £6.50 with sunblush tomatoes, piquillo peppers, aubergine, olives & croutons. Tuk tuk salad £6.50 with wild rice, rocket leaves, toasted seeds and zingy Thai dressing. Organic mezze maniche pasta, sunblush tomato pesto, rocket & pinenuts £6.
Full English vegetarian **breakfast** £6.50. Also pancakes, pastries, toast. There is a free Sunday afternoon classic film in back room at 4.30pm and evening live music.

Fairtrade organic tea and coffee £1.30-2.10, soya milk 30p. Juices and soft drinks £1.30-2.20, some Fairtrade and organic. Wine from £3.25-3.90 glass, £11.80 bottle. Bottled beer and pints from £3.10. Lots of spirits from around £2.
Kids welcome until 21.00, high chairs, board games. Wifi. 4 outside tables. MC, Visa.

King of Hearts
Omnivorous cafe in arts centre

7-15 Fye Bridge, Norwich NR3 1LJ (corner of Fishergate, next to the river)
Tel cafe 01603-620805,
booking office 611412, switchboard 766129
Cafe: Mon-Sat 08.00-16.30, Sun closed;
Centre: Mon-Sat 900-16.00, Sun closed
www.kingofhearts.org.uk

Arts centre in a city centre Tudor building with cafe, craft shop and meeting rooms. Classical music concerts. Free admission to exhibitions. See website for concerts and events.
The cafe uses local produce and has veggie options throughout the menu, some of it vegan or with allergy options. As we write, vegetarian breakfasts are on the way. All soups are veggie or vegan £4.20 with a baguette. Lots of pasta dishes, things with Mediterranean veg, £6.25-7.95. Jacket potato from £4.60, panini and baguettes £4.60 such as hummus with marinated olives and mixed leaves. Food is mostly made to order and they can adapt things for you. Lots of cakes and pastries £1.50-2.20 and they are investigating more vegan options. Fairtrade coffee £1.60-2.60, 14 leaf teas and herb tea £1.50. Soya milk available. Cold drinks, bottled smoothies, Norfolk apple juice £1.40-£2.20. House wine £3.40 glass, £13.95 bottle. Bottled beer £3.20.
Children welcome and they can do smaller portions, 3 high chairs.

Courtyard seating in summer, you can sit outside with your dog. Disabled access and toilet. MC, Visa. Substantial discount for take-away.

Norwich - omnivorous
Norwich Arts Centre
Omnivorous cafe-bar in arts centre

St. Benedict's Street, Norwich, NR2 4PG
Tel: 01603-660352
Cafe-bar open Mon-Sat 10-19.00, lunch served 11.00-16.00, Sun closed
www.norwichartscentre.co.uk

Long established music and events venue with a mostly vegetarian cafe-bar with art on the walls. Eat for £3-£3.75, such as soup of the day and salad of the day, both with bread and usually vegan, veggieburger which is the most popular item, samosas, bhajias, and spring rolls. They're working to improve vegan offerings such as cakes and flapjacks. Teas from 80p, espresso coffee £1.50, soya milk available. Draft and bottled beers and ales, £2.50-3.50. House wine £3 glass, £11 bottle, also organic wines. Children welcome. Wheelchair access. Free internet terminal and wifi. Big garden and shaded courtyard with tables outside. Available for weddings, birthday parties and private hire.

Olives
Omnivorous cafe

40 Elm Hill, Norwich NR3 1HG
Tel: 01603-230500
Open: Mon-Sat 9.00-15.00,
Sun 10.00-15.00
www.olivesnorwich.co.uk

In a cobbled street in the centre. Recommended by local veggies, particularly as breakfast specialists, though not so good for vegan alternatives. Full cooked all day breakfast £5.95 includes mushrooms, root vegetable hash, tomatoes, beans, toast etc, or have something lighter on toast.
Sandwiches, toasties £3.75-4.55 include hummous and red pepper. Specials £4.95-6.95 such as roasted Mediterranean veg and couscous. Desserts and cakes £2.45, but nothing particularly vegan.
Coffee from £1.20, teas £1.30, soya milk available. Beer £2.95, wine from £2.50 glass, £12.50 bottle.
Children welcome, no high chairs. Wheelchair access. 4 comfy sofas to lounge in. Sometimes open for music for music on Friday nights.

Spice Paradise
Omnivorous Indian restaurant

41 Magdalen Street, Norwich NR3 1LQ
Tel: 01603-666601 / 664152
Open: Tue-Fri & Bank Holiday 17.30-23.30;
Sat-Sun 11.30-14.30, 17.30-23.30;
Mon closed except bank holiday
www.norwichspiceparadise.com

Norwich has several Indian restaurants, useful if your mates veto a veggie venue. This one has a vegetarian feast £15.95 with pappadoms, pickles and chutneys, starters, curry selection, side dishes, rice, breads and sweet. Other dishes also include good options for vegans and coeliacs. You can ask for favourites you want included. Licensed.

Norwich - shops
The Greenhouse shop
Vegetarian cafe, take-away & shop

in Norwich's Environment Centre,
42-46 Bethel St, Norwich, NR2 1NR
Tel: 01603-631 007
Open: Tue-Sat 10.00-17.00,
Sun-Mon closed
www.greenhousetrust.co.uk

See page 66.

Rainbow Wholefoods
Vegetarian wholefood shop

Old Fire Station Stables, Labour in Vain Yard, Guildhall Hill, Norwich NR2 1JD
Tel: 01603-625560
Open: Mon-Sat 9.00-18.00, Sun closed
www.rainbowwholefoods.co.uk

100% vegetarian company with a shop in central Norwich since 1976. They champion organic, are totally GM-free and stock over 2,500 products.
Organic fresh bread, fruit and veg, much of it locally grown. Lots of Fairtrade, gluten, dairy, salt and sugar-free. Chilled and frozen organic foods.
Big range of Japanese, macrobiotic and Thai foods including 14 types of seaweed and lots of tofu. 50 kinds of tea.
Bodycare includes Faith in Nature, Bentley Organics, Urtekram, Blue Organics, Weleda. Organic vegan wine and beer.
Food is their main thing, but they do stock supplements and remedies from Cotswold Health, Premier Naturals, Lifestream, Nature's Own, Ricola, Floradix and Helios. Cleaning products by Earth Friendly, Clearspring, BioD, Simply, Footprint, Ecover and refills.
You can eat or have a cuppa in the independently run Pulse vegetarian restaurant upstairs, or outside in the courtyard.

Rainbow Wholesale
Wholefoods wholesale warehouse

Rainbow Wholefoods, White Lodge Estate, Hall Road, Norwich NR4 6DG
Tel: 01603-630484
Fax 01603-664066
Open: Mon-Fri 9.00-16.30
www.rainbowwholefoods.co.uk

Wholesale warehouse supplying their shop in Norwich and many others throughout East Anglia including East of England Coop stores, plus individuals and groups of friends who save money by buying wholefoods and other products in bulk. Over 5,000 vegetarian ethically sourced products. Minimum order £50 for collection, or £200 for free delivery in East Anglia, and they can despatch to anywhere beyond. You must order by 10.30am the working day before, from their website catalogue for registered customers (call or email to register) or you can phone or fax.

The Greengrocers
Greengrocer & omnivorous deli-cafe

Earlham House Shops, Earlham Road, Norwich NR2 3PD. Tel: 01603-250 000
Open: Mon-Sat 08.00-19.00,
Sun 10.00-16.00
www.thegreengrocers.co.uk

70% organic and/or local, the rest is Fairtrade or eco-friendly. Some of the staff are vegan and they specialise in food intolerances. The cafe is mainly vegetarian with just a couple of meat dishes. The shop has a fabulous range of wholefoods and more, though does sell some meat and fish.
Cafe: Vegan soup £3.49 with bread. Pasties £2.99 with salad. Sandwiches such as TLT £2.99 (marinated tofu, lettuce and tomato). Mezze plate £5.95 with sweet garlic, dolmades, salad, hummous, pitta, grilled artichoke. Most desserts £2.99 are vegan such as treacle tart, cakes, Booja Booja ice-cream.
Latte or cappuccino £1.85. 70 types of tea £1.49. Soya milk available.
Children more than welcome, big toy box, high chairs, baby changing. Outside tables where you can sit with your dog. Disabled entries and toilet. Free wifi. Outside catering.
Shop: Huge selection of over 100 types of organic fruit and veg, probably the best selection in the county. Local organic artesan bread. Meat alterna-

tives, tvp, soya, tofu. Lots of vegan milks such as oat, almond, nut milks. Vegan cheeses. Freezer with tempeh, Booja Booja ice-cream. Rice pasta. Gluten-free cakes. Vegan chocolate includes Plamil, Organica and the whole range of Booja Booja. Plamil mayonnaise. Vegan, organic and biodynamic wines, beers and ciders. Yarrah veggie dog food.
Bodycare includes Faith In Nature, Green People, Avalon, Lavera, Urtekram, Weleda, Natracare. Nature baby care, Maltex, Ella's Kitchen. Viridian supplements.
BioD, Earth Friendly and Ecover (plus refills) cleaning products. Some health and cook books, cards and gifts. Occasionally there is a nutritionist in the shop, and sometimes Friday morning health and wellbeing talks. MC, Visa.

Norwich - shops
Wholefood Planet
Wholefood shop & cafe

Units C & D, Yarefield Park, Old Hall Road, Norwich NR4 6FF (south Norwich, off the A140 Ipswich Rd, turn at Holiday Inn into Hall Road then Old Hall Rd)
Tel: 01603-457 093
Open: Mon-Sat 9.00-17.30, Sun closed
www.wholefoodplanet.com/norwich

New wholefood store opened Jan 2009, based on the model of Daily Bread in Cambridge and Northampton. Organic and local wholefoods, fruit and veg, Fairtrade and ethically sourced products.
Chillers with pies, pasties, tofu, vegan cheese and meat substitutes. Booja Booja, Organica and Plamil vegan chocolate. Gluten-free foods.
Bodycare includes Faith In Nature, Lavera, Toms and Suma, Natracare. Lots of baby stuff. Ecover and refills. and nappies. Health books.
Cafe with tea £1.20, coffee £1.50, soya milk available. Cakes, with vegan and gluten-free on the way.

They don't have plastic bags but sell hessian shopping bags and can give you a cardboard box. Local noticeboard. Car park, disabled access, Changing Places toilet. MC, Visa.

Lush, Norwich
Vegetarian cosmetics shop

30 Gentleman's Walk, Norwich NR2 1NA
Tel: 01603-627 615
Open Mon-Sat 9.00-18.00, Thu till 19.00, Sun 10.00-17.00
www.lush.co.uk

Fun things to relax with in the bathroom of your B&B or at home such as foaming bath balls. Almost all products are vegan and clearly labelled as such.

Sheringham
The All Natural Company
Health food shop

30A High St, Sheringham NR26 8JR
Tel: 01263-825881
Open: Mon-Sat summer 9.30-17.00, winter 16.30; Sun closed
www.sheringhamtown.co.uk/allnatural.htm

Local bread, some with local flour, some organic. Fridge with vegan cheeses, Taisun meat substitutes, burgers. Freezer with Swedish Glace. Plamil chocolate, plus other brands at Christmas. Baby foods.
Bodycare includes local Sorrells, Eccobella and Sante makeup, Jason, Faith In Nature, Avalon, Dead Sea Magik, Natracare. Nature Babycare and Earth Friendly baby things. Ecover.
Supplements include Nature's Aid, Nature's Own, Solgar, Vogel, Biohealth, FSC. Nelsons, New Era and Weleda homeopathy. Absolute Aromas essential oils. Sometimes there are practitioners giving taster sessions in the shop such as nutritionist, reflexology, Reiki. MC, Visa over £5.

Swaffham

The Green Parrot
Health food shop

Montpelier House, 89 Market Place, Swaffham PE37 7AQ. Tel: 01760-724704
Open: Mon-Fri 9.30-17.00, Sat 9.00-16.30, Sun closed

Fridge with tofu and vegan cheeses. Local handmade additive-free bread. Freezer with Realeat mince, tvp, Fry's/Beanies, Swedish Glace. Vegan chocolate by Plamil, Divine, Booja Booja. Bodycare includes local company Essential Care, Barefoot Botanicals, Weleda, Faith In Nature, Green People, Green Things, BWC cosmetics, Natracare. Earth Friendly baby range, Maltex. Full range of homeopathic and flower remedies, essential oils. Ecover and refills.
Supplements include Solgar, Biocare, Biohealth, Viridian, Nature's Aid, Higher Nature, Bioforce (A.Vogel), Health Aid.
Clinic upstairs with two homeopaths, chiropracter, osteopath, two acupuncturists, masseur, nutritional therapist, hypnotherapist and counsellor.
They also do mail order.

Walsham

Health Food Centre
Health food shop

27 Market Place, North Walsham NR28 9BS
Tel: 01692-403219
Open: Wed Sat 9-4, Mon-Fri 9-5, Sun closed

Gluten-free bread. Fridge with vegan cheeses, tofu, meat substitutes. Freezer with veggie sausages, bacon, Swedish Glace. Plamil chocolate.
Bodycare includes Jason, Weleda, Natracare. Bach flower remedies. Lots of aromatherapy. Supplements include Nature's Aid, Lifeplan, Bioforce, Lanes, Quest. Ecover and refills.

Wymondham

Wymondham Health Foods
Health food shop

17 Market Street, Wymondham NR18 0AJ
Tel: 01953-603738
Open: Mon-Fri 8.30-17.30, Sat 17.00, Sun closed

Open since 1983. Fridge with tofu, vegan cheeses, Freezer with lots of Realeat, Goodlife, Vegetarian's Choice, Linda McCartney, Swedish Glaces cornets. Dry tvp. Vegan chocolate by Montezuma and Plamil.
Bodycare includes Jason, Weleda, Faith In Nature, Natracare. Maltex nappies. Supplements mainly by Solgar, Nature's Aid, A.Vogel. Weleda homeopathy, Bach flower remedies, Natural by Nature essential oils. Ecover and refills for laundry and washing up. MC, Visa.

Chain stores

Holland & Barrett
Health food shop

31 Market Place, **Great Yarmouth** NR30 1LX
Tel: 01493-858226
Open: Mon-Sat 9.00-5.30, Sun 10.00-16.00

15 Norfolk Street, **Kings Lynn** PE30 1AR
Tel: 01553-765 969
Open: Mon-Sat 9.00-17.30, Sun 10-16.00

19/21 White Lion Street, **Norwich** NR2 1QA
Tel: 01603-762 955
Open: Mon-Sat 9.00-5.30, Thu till 20.00, Sun 10.30-4.30

Local group

Norfolk Vegetarian & Vegan Society
www.vegfolk.co.uk

Kelmarsh	75
Northampton	75
Rushden	77
Towcester	77
Wellingborough	77
Wymington	78
Chain stores	78

Northamptonshire

Leafcycles
Fruit & veg delivery & accommodation

Blackcurrent Centre, 24 St Michaels Ave, Northampton NN1 4JQ (off Kettering Road)
Tel: 01604-628956
www.leafcycles.co.uk
www.blackcurrentcentre.org.uk

Founded in 1995, Leafcycles is Northampton's original organic veg box delivery scheme, a non-profit making community enterprise run by a workers' co-operative, based in the Blackcurrent Centre for environment and social change. They deliver organic fruit & veg set boxes, packed at a local farm, straight to your home or workplace all over Northampton and sometimes beyond, using bicycles and trailers. Large box £11.50 contains about 10 veg varieties.
Blackcurrent is a vegan and vegetarian housing co-op and usually has space for people to stay, £8 per night, phone for more info.

Rushden
Health Foods & Home Brew
Health food shop with homebrew kits

71 High Street, Rushden NN10 0QE
Tel: 01933-355048
Open: Mon-Sat 9.00-17..00, Sun closed
www.healthfoodandhomebrews.co.uk

Fridge with dairy-free cheese, Provamel desserts and yogurts. Sugar and gluten-free foods. Bodycare includes Aubrey Organics, Avalon, Dead Sea Magik. Supplements include Nature's Aid, Solgar, A Vogel and Weleda. Weleda homeopathy. Natural by Nature aromatherapy. Occasionally they have a homeopath in for the day.
Big range of home brew kits for beer and wine.

Towcester
The Health Pot
Health food shop

11 Sponne Shopping Centre, Watling Street, Towcester NN12 6BY (Market town 12 miles north of Milton Keynes on A5 to Luton and Dunstable). Tel: 01327-358700
Open: Mon-Fri 9.30-17.00, Sat 9.00-15.00, Sun closed
www.healthpot.co.uk

Usual wholefoods. Fridge with vegan cheeses, meat substitutes. No freezer. Plamil vegan chocolate.
Bodycare includes Faith In Nature, Jason, Weleda, Natracare.
Supplements include Solgar, Viridian, Nature's Plus especially children's, sports nutrition. Helios homeopathy. Absolute Aromas essential oils. Ecover and refills. MC, Visa.

Wellingborough
Pooja
Vegetarian Indian restaurant & shop

33 Alma Street, Wellingborough NN8 4DH
Tel: 01933-278 800
Open: Tue-Sun 12.00-22.00
www.poojacaterers.co.uk/restaurant.htm

Catering business, followed by a restaurant and Indian sweet shop, founded by two Indian brothers in 1991. Punjabi, Gujarati and South Indian food for £3.50-4.75 per dish. £10-12 for a meal. Thalis £5.50, £7.50. House wine £9.50 bottle, £2.50 glass. Children welcome, high chair. MC, Visa. Outside catering.

EAST Northamptonshire

Wellingborough

Wellingborough Health Foods
Health food shop

22 Silver Street, Wellingborough NN8 1AY
Tel: 01933-222499
Open: Mon-Sat 9.00-17.30, Sun closed

Fridge and freezer with vegan cheeses, meat substitutes, Swedish Glace. Bodycare includes Weleda, Dead Sea Magik, Faith in Nature, Jason. Natracare women's personal care. Ecover cleaning products. Books and Kindred Spirit magazine.
Wide selection of supplements. Remedies and homeopathy. Intolerance and sensitivity testing. Sometimes a qualified nutritionist from a manufacturer is in the shop for free consultations.
Fortnightly delivery service to surrounding towns – call and they'll send you full details.

Wymington

The New Inn
Omnivorous pub-restaurant

Rushden Road, Wymington, Beds NN10 9LN (on the outskirts of Rushden about a mile from the A6, 8 miles north of Bedford.)
Tel: 01933-317618
Pub open: 7 days 12.00-24.00
Food Wed-Sat 12.00-14.0, 18.00-21.00;
Sun lunch 12.00-15.00, no food Tue

On Northants/Beds border. See Bedfordshire chapter for menu and prices. Children and dogs welcome. Games room.

Chain stores

Holland & Barrett
Health food shop

43 Queens Square, **Corby** NN17 1PD
Tel: 01536-408 914

Unit 8, The Newlands, **Kettering** NN16 8JL
Tel: 01536-411341

25 Abington Street, **Northampton** NN1 2AN
Tel: 01604-634270

Julian Graves
Health food shop

47 Abington Street, **Northampton** NN1 2AW
Tel: 01604-414377
Open: Mon-Sat 9.30-17.00, Sun 10-16.00

Billing Garden Centre, The Causeway, **Great Billing**, Northampton NN3 9EX
Tel: 01604-414377
Open: Mon-Sat 9.30 17.00, Sun 10.00-16.00

43 Spring Lane, Swansgate Shopping Centre, **Wellingborough** NN8 1EY
Tel: 01933-443487
Open: Mon-Sat 9.00-17.30, Sun closed

Tourist information:
www.northamptonshiretouristguide.com
www.northamptonshire.co.uk
www.explorenorthamptonshire.co.uk

Suffolk

If Norwich is the new Brighton (cute streets and loads of veggie cafes) then Suffolk is the new West Country and much closer to London, ideal for a city-zen wind down weekend. There are six veggie places to stay, several veggie cafes, and excellent country pub-restaurants including the fabulous **The Red Lion**, East Anglia's only 100% vegetarian pub. (There are 10 more veggie pubs in *Vegetarian Britain*) Don't miss the new veggie wine bar and restaurant **The Cross** in Woodbridge, opened Nov 2009. The county has many fine independent wholefood stores.

Accommodation	79	Lowestoft	87
Beccles	82	Mildenhall	87
Bungay	82	Newmarket	87
Bury St. Edmunds	83	Southwold	87
Debenham	84	Stowmarket	88
Great Bricett	84	Sudbury	88
Hadleigh	85	Woodbridge	88
Halesworth	85	Chain stores	89
Hoxne	85	Local group	89
Ipswich	85		

Suffolk - accommodation

Old Hall, Barsham

99% vegetarian B&B with self-catering annex & camping

2 The Old Hall, Barsham, **Beccles**. NR34 8HB
Tel: 01502-714661. Open: all year
Train: Beccles 2.5 miles then taxi 01502-710999. Directions: 2 miles west of Beccles. Take the B1062 towards Bungay and turn right onto track signed "Callendars Houses". Continue down track for half a mile.
www.bikeways.org.uk
graham@bikeways.org.uk

Organic smallholding producing much of their our own food, in the peaceful Waveney Valley in the Broads National Park, half a mile from the nearest road. Food is seasonal and organic, and all bought-in food is organic. Not a mainstream B&B so visit their website to see if it is what you are looking for. They are into food preservation (bottling, drying, juice, wine), spinning, dyeing, knitting, cycling, yoga, massage, green living.

Bed and breakfast for up to 15 in twin, double and family rooms, £20 per person. No single supplement. Self catering for up to 8 in bunk beds £100 first night, £35 subsequent nights. Camping £1 per person per night. £5 per car per night. Homemade organic sourdough bread, organic cereals, homemade organic apple juice and other seasonal food. Evening meal £7. Can easily cater for vegans. The owners are 99% vegetarian but do eat the cockerels from their egg-laying chickens. No smoking throughout. Children welcome. Cycle friendly. No tv, wifi, pets or credit cards.

20 minutes walk across the marshes is **Geldeston Locks Inn**, a music and real ale/cider pub with a garden on the Norfolk side of the River Waveney between Beccles and Bungay. They have beanburgers and veggie goulash. See www.geldestonlocks.co.uk. No credit cards.

Rainbow Bed & Breakfast

New vegetarian B&B in the middle of East Anglia, an ideal base for exploring, or come for a Chill-out & Detox retreat weekend.

4 en suite rooms: 1 single £36-39; large double £35-40 per person with very large super duper bed, seating area and desk; ground floor twin £35-38 with seating area and desk; ground floor family suite sleeps 4 adults £30-38 each, plus 1 child on guest bed. Single in double room minimum £45. Discount for more than 7 days.

Continental breakfast includes juices, fruit, (soya) yoghurts, cereals (organic, wheat or gluten-free), nuts and seeds, organic bread/toast, normal or gluten-free croissants, muffins, crumpets, cereal bars. Organic teas, coffees, herbal and fruit infusions. Soya milk, vegan margarine and muesli available. Breakfast can be in the garden in summer, or in your room.

In-house therapy room offering reflexology, aromatherapy, deep tissue massage, allergy testing and stress management consultations. There is a large, intriguing garden to explore or relax in. There are lots of walks and excellent cycle routes.

The cathedral and historic market town of Bury St Edmunds is 4 miles away, and nearby is Ickworth House and Gardens. It is 15 minutes to West Stow Country Park & Anglo-Saxon Village, or Lackford Lakes & Nature Reserve; 20 mins to Thetford Forest or Lavenham; 30 to Newmarket or Ipswich; 35 to Cambridge or Felixstowe Beach; 45 to Norwich.

The local garden centre Harveys Plants has a good veggie option. In Bury there is the fantastic Butterworths independent health food store, and Holland & Barrett has a vegetarian cafe. Cambridge has the renowned veggie restaurant Rainbow Cafe and Ipswich has a veggie cafe and some veggie-friendly restaurants.

Thurston

Vegetarian bed & breakfast & retreats

27 Barton Road
Thurston
Bury-St-Edmunds
Suffolk IP31 3PA

Tel: 01359-233133
Mobile: 07803 128704

www.rainbowbedandbreakfast.co.uk

Email: julie@rainbowbedandbreakfast.co.uk

Train: Thurston 3-5mins walk. Regular train, bus & taxi service. They can also collect.

Open: all year

Directions: From A14 take junction 46 to Thurston & Beyton. Follow road through Beyton Village into Thurston, under railway bridge, left at mini-roundabout. This is Barton Road and they are on the left.

Parking for 6 cars

Can cater for diabetic, coeliac etc.

Children all ages welcome, high chair, travel cot

No smoking throughout

Rooms have TV, bottled water and organic, Fairtrade tea/coffee making, complimentary toiletries and bodycare they make themselves with no SLS or parabens. Wifi.

White House Farm

New B&B in traditional rural farmhouse at the edge of an organic wildlife site. The farm is an idyllic place to stay in the heart of Suffolk, located down quiet winding country lanes. Guests can explore the wildlife site with wildflower meadows, ancient hedgerows and woodland. There are many other walks and excellent cycle routes.

One double £70 (single occupancy £50), one large double 4-poster room £90 (single £70) and a gypsy caravan £70 (single £50) set in a picturesque meadow. All bedrooms overlook the farmhouse garden and woodland.

Breakfasts are served in an Arts and Crafts summerhouse and include organic, Fairtrade, local and homemade produce. The menu includes organic Fairtrade tea, coffee and herbal teas, croissants, wholemeal toast, organic/local preserves, organic porridge, fruit compote, local farm-pressed apple juice, fresh fruit and cereals. Soya milk, vegan margarine and cereal are available. Breakfast in room if ordered evening before.

White House Farm is just 3 miles from the centre of Woodbridge, a picturesque market town at the edge of the River Deben estuary. It has many historic pubs, restaurants and independent shops. There are many veggie-friendly pubs and restaurants nearby including The Cherry Tree, Strawberry Café and Prezzo at Woodbridge. The Dog Inn at nearby Grundisburgh also has good veggie options. There is an excellent farm shop in the village and health food shops in nearby towns including Woodbridge.

The farm is 15 minutes to the Anglo-Saxon burial site at Sutton Hoo and 25 minutes to Framlingham Castle, Snape Maltings and Ipswich. Aldeburgh, Orford Castle, Flatford Mill, Minsmere and Dunwich on the coast are all about 35-45 minutes drive.

Woodbridge

Vegetarian bed & breakfast

White House Farm
Hasketon, Woodbridge
Suffolk IP13 6JP

Tel: 01394-382992

www.sinfieldtrust.org then click on B&B link

Email: info@sinfieldtrust.org

Train: Woodbridge 3 miles, . regular trains direct from London. Then bus or taxi.

Open: all year

Directions: From A12 turn at Grundisburgh/Woodbridge roundabout onto B1079 towards Grundisburgh. Take first right towards Hasketon then first left onto Blacksmith Rd. Follow this into Hasketon village. After church on left the road bends sharply to the right at a brick wall. After this bend take second left opposite Highfield House. White House Farm is 1/3 mile on the right.

Parking next to house

No dogs as they have friendly cats

No smoking throughout

Rooms have tea/coffee making with organic and Fairtrade products & natural toiletries. Hairdryers.

10% discount to people presenting this book

See photo on front cover

Suffolk - accommodation
Western House
Vegetarian bed and breakfast

High Street, **Cavendish**, Suffolk CO10 8AR
Tel: 01787-280 550
Train station: Sudbury 7 miles
Open: all year
www.suffolktouristguide.com/Cavendish.asp

One single, one double and two twins at £20-£22 per person. Vegans catered for with prior notice. Children aged 2 onwards welcome. No pets (they have cats). No smoking throughout. There are Indian restaurants in Long Melford (3 miles) and Clare (3 miles the other way) with good vegetarian food.

Holly Tree House
Vegetarian bed and breakfast

Bleach Green, **Wingfield**, near Diss IP21 5RG
Tel: 01379-384068
Train station: Diss 10 miles
www.hollytreehousebandb.co.uk
hb.challinor@googlemail.com

17th century timber framed house with later additions on the Suffolk/Norfolk borders. 2 double ensuite rooms £32.50 per person, or £42.50 single. No smoking or pets, not suitable for small children. They have a friendly dog.

Swallow Organics
Holiday cottage and fruit & veg stall

High March, Darsham, **Saxmundham**, IP17 3RN.
Tel: 01728-668 201 (1-2pm or after 7pm)
Train station: Darsham 1 mile
Open: all year
Stall: summer 9.00-17.00 daily except Tue; winter Wed-Sat 9.00-dusk

Vegetarian owned organic smallholding, next to Westleton Suffolk heritage coast, with an old-fashioned cottage. The 3.5 acres of organic fruit and veg produce a wide range of produce and they organise vegetable boxes for collection. You can place an order or buy from their stall at the front (closed Tue in summer, closed Sun-Tue in winter).
The cottage sleeps two adults, £260 per week April to end September, £220 Oct to March. Adults only as they have too many ponds. Dogs welcome.

Beccles
Hungate Health Store
Health food shop

4 Hungate, Beccles, Suffolk NR34 9TL
Tel: 01502-715009
Open: Mon-Fri 9.00-17.15, Wed 9.00-16.00, Sat 9.00-17.00, Sun closed

Fridge and freezer with vegan Sheese and Cheezely, Redwood meat substitutes, tofu, Booja Booja and Swedish Glace. Metfield local bakery organic bread. Bodycare includes Essential Care (very good for people with sensitive skin), Dead Sea Magik, Avalon, Faith In Nature, Natracare. Lots of supplements including Solgar, Bioforce. Weleda homeopathy. Some essential oils. Beer and wine-making kits.

Bungay
The Little Green Wholefood Shop
Wholefood shop

39/41 Earsham Street, Bungay, Suffolk NR35 1AF (6 miles west of Beccles)
Tel: 01986-894555
Open: Mon-Sat 9.00-17.30, Sun closed
www.bungay-suffolk.co.uk/wholefood.htm

Organic fuit and veg. Metfield Bakery and All Natural organic bread, spelt, rye etc. Fridge includes spinach wraps, vegan cheeses and meat substitutes. Freezer with frozen fruit, veg, butternut

squash roast, beanburgers, Swedish Glace and Booja Booja. Vegan chocolate by Montezuma and Booja Booja. Organic and local wine.
Bodycare by Faith In Nature, Avalon, Weleda, Natracare. Faith In Nature, Weleda and Earth Friendly Baby. Homeopathy, herbal remedies.
Supplements include Solgar, Nature's Aid, Vogel. Cleaning products by Faith In Nature, Ecoleaf, Ecover and some refills. Health books and free magazines. Therapy room upstairs with arts therapy etc. Occasionally a nutritionist. MC, Visa.

Bury St. Edmunds
Holland & Barrett Cafe
Vegetarian cafe in health food shop

6 Brentgrovel Street, Bury St. Edmunds IP33 1EA. Tel: 01284-706 677
Cafe: Mon-Tue, Thu-Fri 10.00-15.00
Wed 9.30-16.00, Sat 9.30-16.00
Shop: Mon-Sat 9.00-17.30, Sun 11.00-15.00

Jacket potatoes £3.50-4.05 with salad. Wholemeal sandwiches £2.95, add 50p for toastie, they can use dairy-free cheeses in anything. Goblin vegetarian, vegan and gluten-free meals. 4 or 5 specials around £4.50 for a main meal changes weekly, such as risotto. Vegan gluten-free soup £3.50 with bread. Sausage on mash with caramelised onion and gravy. Things on toast. Coffee £1-1.50. Tea and teacake £1.80. Cake from 70p, vegan gluten-free apricot and date slices 70p.
Number of vegan dishes: approx. 1.
Items are labeled as vegan on the menu. Vegans will be better catered with notice.
Good for kids though no high chairs. Customer toilet. Patio doors to a courtyard garden that you can sit in.
Shop has bread, chiller with pates, porkless pies, vegan cheeses, slices and cakes. In the old part of town, the coffee shop has oldey worldey beams.

Market days are Wed and Fri with fruit and veg.

The Linden Tree
Omnivorous English restaurant-pub

7 Out Northgate, Bury St. Edmunds IP33 1JQ (near the train station)
Tel: 01284-754 600
Open: Mon-Sun 12-23.00, Sat from 11.00.
Food Mon-Fri 12.00-14.30, 18.00-21.30;
Sat 12.00-21.30; Sun 12-15.00, 17-20.00
www.lindentreenorthgate.co.uk

Listed building stone-built pub on the outskirts of town. with food cooked to order. The menu has at least 5 vegetarian mains daily £8.99, plus 1 veggie special £7.99 such as korma curry with rice and naan. They always have something vegan or can fix it for you. There is also a second lighter lunch menu that runs alongside the main menu until 14.30, Sat till 17.00, but not on Sundays, with filled rolls to order from £4.25 on ciabatta, French or granary with side salad; jacket potatoes from £4.99. Desserts £4.50 are all dairy based but vegans can ask for a fruit salad. Children's menu £4.95, high chairs, baby changing.
House wine £2.90-3.70 glass. Wine from £9.99 bottle. Big garden with seating. Dogs welcome in garden. Visa, MC.

Butterworths Health Food & Herbs
Health food and herbs shop

9 The Traverse, Bury St. Edmunds IP33 1BJ
Tel: 01284-755410
Open: Mon-Sat 9.00-17.30, Sun closed
www.butterworths-healthfoods.co.uk

Specialists in Chinese, Indian, Philippines and Asian foods such as cassava, many types of fresh chillies, spices, karela, exotic mushrooms. Local sourdough breads such as spelt on

Fridays. Fridge and freezer have sprouts, vegan cheeses, spreads, Booja Booja. Tartex and other pates. Plamil vegan chocolate, Booja Booja truffles. Lots of teas and coffees.
Bodycare by Green People, Weleda, Faith In Nature, Natracare. Weleda Baby, and sun creams in summer. Ecoleaf and Ecover cleaning.
Supplements include Solgar, Higher Nature, Biohealth, Weleda, Nelsons and Vogel. Weleda homeopathy, remedies and advice. Essential oils. Nutrition and diet advice. One of the owners is qualified in holistic therapies and nutrition.
Wine and beer homebrew kits, all you need in a box or they can sell you anything from a single cork to a real oak barrel and advise you how to use up your surplus fruit crop.
They make gift baskets for you in seagrass or cane, can create hampers, and have gift bags for loose teas and coffees. MC, Visa minimum £5.

Debenham

Dove Valley

Organic shop & box scheme

2 Chancery Lane, Debenham IP14 6RN (east of Stowmarket) Tel: 01728-861258 www.dovevalley.co.uk

Local organic and Fairtrade groceries, gluten-free, vegetarian and vegan. Fruit and veg bag delivery.
It is next to the Co-op which has a good range of vegan chilled necessities for a village shop.

Great Bricett

The Red Lion

Vegetarian pub

Greenstreet Green, Great Bricett, Suffolk, IP7 7DD. Tel: 01473-657799
Pub open Tue-Sun 12.00-14.30, food till 14.00; evenings 18.00-23.00, food till 21.00 or 20.30 on Sundays; Mon closed.
Directions: On the B1078 roughly halfway between Needham Market and Bildeston. Stay on the main road and you will find it about 200 yards past the turning to the village(coming from Needham).
From A14 get off at Junction 51 at the bottom of the A140. Follow the signs into Needham, and then to Bildeston.
www.theveggieredlion.co.uk (menu)

Fantastic! A vegetarian country pub, about 30 minutes from Bury St Edmunds and 20 minutes from Ipswich. One of our researchers says the quality of the food is fabulous and worth a big detour for. Menu changes frequently. Starters could include £4.90 avocado salad; sweet potato soup with chilli oil and toasted almonds. Light meals £7.90 such as Thai yellow curry or Mexican chimichangas (vegan option). Main course £9.90 such as African sweet potato stew; Mediterranean vegetable and tomato pie. Specials board changes weekly, for example main course of walnut salad with brown rice, pear and avocado. Desserts £3.90 include vegan summer pudding with dairy-free ice-cream, or sorbet in a chocolate basket (suitable for vegans). Give them a call if you have any special dietary requirements.
Wine from £2.85 glass, £10.90 bottle.
Dogs ok in bar area and they can sit outside on the outside patio which has tables, and there are further picnic tables on the grass. Kids welcome, menu can be adapted. Baby changing facilities. Al fresco terrace. Can cater functions up to 30 people.

Hadleigh
Sunflower
Health food shop

101 High Street, Hadleigh, Suffolk IP7 5EJ
Tel: 01473-823219
Open: Mon-Fri 9.00-17.30 (Wed till 13.00),
Sat 9.00-16.00, Sun closed
www.sunflowerhealth.co.uk

Fridge and freezer with Bute Island Sheese, Swedish Glace, Booja Booja, Beanies. Organic, gluten-free, sugar-free foods. Sourdough bread. Faith In Nature shower gels and shampoos, Tom's and rock deodorants. Supplements including Solgar, Nature's Aid, Bioforce, Biohealth. Flower remedies, Weleda homeopathy, essential oils. Ecover cleaning. Books and magazines.

Halesworth
Focus Organic
Organic food shop

14 Thoroughfare, Halesworth IP19 8AH
Tel: 01986-872899
Open: Mon-Sat 9.00-17.30, Sun closed
www.focusorganic.co.uk

Bread and baked goods. Delicatessen with savoury slices, spring rolls, olives, bottled sauces, condiments. Organic veg delivered Friday. Dry goods including flour and cereals, teas, coffees. Lots of sugar-free biscuits, chocolates, snack bars, jams. Lots of gluten-free. Green People, Jason and Lavera, Weleda, Toms bodycare. Organic vegetarian wine. Wide range of vitamins. Health books. Next door are ethical clothing, Fairtrade, bags, gifts and accessories.

Hoxne
The Swan Inn
Pub & restaurant

Low Street, Hoxne, Eye, Suffolk IP21 5AS
(5 mins from Eye, 9 mins from Diss on B1118)
Tel: 01379-668275
Open: every day 12.00-15.00, 18.00-23.00
Food till 21.00
www.hoxneswan.co.uk

Grade II listed real ale pub dating back to 1480 on the Norfolk border in the beautiful village of Hoxne. Open fires. Home-made bread. Wide choice of veggie dishes, starter size £5-6, main £8.95-10.95 such as chilli bean. They cook mainly to order so can veganise dishes. Glass of wine from £3.25, bottle £11.50. Well behaved children welcome. Large garden. Dogs on leads welcome in the bar, water and biscuits available. MC, Visa.

Ipswich - vegetarian
Museum Street Cafe
Vegetarian cafe

Westgate House, Museum St, Ipswich IP1 1HQ
Tel: 01473-232393
Open: Mon-Fri 8.30-16.30, Sat-Sun closed
www.museumstreetcafe.com

Hooray, Ipswich finally has a lovely new vegetarian cafe, and they aim to offer vegan options every day too. They operate on the canteen principle with hot food ready to serve on a hot-plate so that people who work locally or are in a hurry can grab a meal. They use local ingredients where possible and buy from ethical wholesalers such as Suma. Great value too with main courses under £5 including a green salad, and plenty more salads are available as extras. Mains include various tarts, sweet potato cakes, lentil patties with home-made chutneys, spinach roulade etc.

Ploughman's includes home-made pickles, hummus and pitta bread with sun-dried tomato salad, vegans can have extra hummus or something else. Soups, usually vegan, served from autumn to late spring.
Home-made cakes, some vegan such as orange and date, from 70p for a choc slice to £1.70 for a large slice of cake. Mug of tea £1, small pot £1.50, large pot £2.30. Coffee, cappuccino etc £1.20-1.95. Soya milk available.
Children welcome, and next door is the Real Nappy Network shop with baby changing facilities and can lend a high chair. One small outside table. Not licensed, corkage may be charged. No credit cards. Sometimes open in the evening for backgammon or other activities

Ipswich – continued

Kwan Thai
Omnivorous Thai restaurant

14 St. Nicholas Street, Ipswich IP1 1TJ
Tel: 01473-253 106
Open: every day 12-14.00,
18-23.00 (Sat till 23.30)
www.kwan-thai-restaurant.freeserve.co.uk

Separate vegetarian sections on the menu. Dishes cooked to order so they can vary set menus. 9 soups and starters £3.25-4.95, or have a selection of 4 for 2 people £11.75 with spring rolls, crispy fried pasta, sweetcorn and mix veg. 13 veggie mains £3.95-£5.50 include bean curd with Chinese black mushroom, sweet and sour stir-fry veg, peanut curry. 4 set menus £15.50-16.25 per person (minimum 2) include sweet and sour panang, stir fried mushrooms and sweetcorn, red or green curry, phad thai and steamed rice. Children welcome, high chair. House wine £3.55 glass, £11.95-12.95 bottle. MC, Visa. Take-away 10% off.

My Keralam
Omnivorous South Indian restaurant

24 St. Helens Street, Ipswich IP4 1HJ
Tel: 01473-288599
Open: Mon-Sat 12.00-14.30, 17.30-23.00,
Sun 12.00-23.00
www.keralamrestaurant.co.uk

Ipswich Food Co-op tells us this place is amazing, all the local veggies go there. Veg platter of starters £8.95 for two people. Dosas £5.45, curries around £3.95 per dish, pooris and iddlis £4.95. Lunch thali £5.95. They tell us the gulab jamun is vegan £2.95.
Wine £11 bottle, £3.95 glass. Children welcome, no high chairs.

Ipswich Food Co-op
Vegetarian & organic wholefood coop

Tel: 01473-684449
Open: Alternate Saturdays 10.00-14.00
www.ipswichfoodcoop.co.uk
info@ipswichfoodcoop.co.uk

In the absence of any independent wholefood shops in Ipswich, this was set up by locals. Run for and by its members, they meet every 2 weeks on a Saturday to collect vegetarian and organic wholefoods, locally or ethically sourced. At the time of printing they have just moved the meetings to the Citizens Advice Bureau at 19 Tower St, in the centre of town behind the bus station. They add just 5% onto the wholesale price of goods to members. Members weigh out their own goods and look up the price from a list. Bring old washing up bottles for liquids. You can just turn up or place bulk orders for anything in the Suma catalogue and various local producers. They have info about box schemes for fruit and veg.
Also a Fairtrade **cafe** facility, so shopping becomes a sociable, relaxed affair. They also run workshops and hold feasts.

Lowestoft
Holland & Barrett Cafe
Vegetarian cafe in health food shop

17 The Britton Centre, Lowestoft NR32 1LR
Tel: 01502-500 832
Open: Cafe upstairs Mon Wed 10-16.00,
Thu-Sat 9.30-16.30, Sun closed.
Shop Mon-Sat, 9-17.30, Sun 10-16.30

Coffee shop similar menu to the one in Bury St Edmunds but cheaper prices. Substantial main meal £5.20 such as salad with jacket potato and mixed bean casserole; or mushroom pilaf with salad. Pasties £1.40. Filled jacket potatoes £2.80-3.60. Beans on toast £2.50. Soup £3.10 with roll. Sandwiches £2.30-2.50, soya spread available. Tea or coffee £1.15, latte etc from £1.60, soya milk available. Coffee with cake £1.70. High chair. Customer toilet.
Shop has fridge with take-away food and freezer.

Oregano Health Foods
Health food shop

169-171 London Road North, Lowestoft NR32 1HG. Tel: 01502-582907
Open: Tue-Sat 8.30-17.00, Sun-Mon closed

Fridge and freezer with vegan cheeses and meat substitutes, Swedish Glace. Bodycare includes Weleda, Jason, Avalon, Urtekram, Faith In Nature. Ecover cleaning. Supplements, homeopathy, aromatherapy.

Mildenhall
The Judes Ferry
Omnivorous pub & restaurant

Judes Ferry, Ferry Lane, West Row, Mildenhall, Suffolk IP28 8PT. (West Row village is just outside Mildenhall, 14 miles NW of Bury St Edmunds) Tel: 01638-712277
Open: Pub hours all day, shut afternoon Mon-Thur. Food lunch and evening till 9pm.

www.judesferry.co.uk

Traditional village riverside pub with large garden and seating by the river. Lunchtime vegetarian baguettes £5.95. Cooked meals change regularly, lunchtime £8.95, evening £9.25-12.95, such as deep fried tofu veg stir-fry, curry, chilli, wild mushroom risotto. Can cater for vegans and gluten-free.
Wine from £2.80 glass, £9.95 bottle. 2 or 3 real ales. Children welcome, high chairs. Dogs welcome in the garden. Parking. MC, Visa.

Newmarket
Pizza Express, Newmarket
Omnivorous Italian restaurant

75 High Street, Newmarket CB8 8NA
Tel: 01638-664 646
Open: Mon-Sun 11.30-23.00
www.pizzaexpress.com

See Bedford for menu.

Southwold
Focus Organic
Organic food shop

76 High Street, Southwold, Suffolk IP18 6DN
Tel: 01502-725299
Open: Mon-Sat 9.00-17.00 (closed 16.00 on Wed in winter), Sun 11.00-16.00, sometimes open later in summer or if busy
www.focusorganic.co.uk

Fridge with soft drinks, tofu, vegan yogurt and cheeses. Bread. Dry goods including flour and cereals, teas, coffees. Lots of sugar-free biscuits, chocolates, snack bars, jams and they cater for coeliacs, lots of gluten-free. Lots of cosmetics and makeup. Health books. Wide range of vitamins.
This branch has an **Ice-cream counter** with dairy-free vegan, gluten-free, sugar-free to take away, organic and gluten-free cones.

Stowmarket
Holland & Barrett Cafe
Vegetarian cafe in health food shop

8/10 Market Place, Stowmarket IP14 1DP
Tel: 01449-676 046
Open: Mon-Sat cafe upstairs 9.30-15.30, shop downstairs 8.30-17.00; Sun closed

Coffee shop similar menu to the one in Bury St Edmunds but cheaper prices. Lunch specials £2.65 and there is always something vegan such as pilaf. Filled jacket potatoes from £3.15. Beans on toast £2.10. Soup £2.99. Sandwiches from £2.05, toastie £2.19. Tea or coffee £1.09. Coffee with teacake £1.65. Good for kids, high chair. Customer toilet. Shop has a fridge but no freezer.

Sudbury
Golden Harvest Health Foods
Vegetarian health food shop

96 North Street, Sudbury CO10 1RF
Tel: 01787-376214
Open: Mon-Sat 9.00-17.00, Sun closed
www.goldenharvest.org.uk

Fridge and freezer with Goblins savoury slices, pinto pies, veg samosas, pastries and cakes (some vegan), vegan cheeses, meat substitutes, Swedish Glace. Fresh bread. Sugar-free and gluten-free. Bodycare includes Avalon and Faith In Nature, Natracare women's care. Supplements by Solgar and A Vogel. Herbatint hair colours. Aromatherapy oils, base oils, burners. Health and alternative therapy books.
North Street natural health clinic at the same address with beauty therapy, counselling and anger management, Reiki, shiatsu, reflexology.

Woodbridge
The Cross
Vegetarian restaurant & wine bar

2 Church Street, Woodbridge IP12 1DH
Tel: 01394-389076
Open: Tue-Sat 12.00-15.00, 18.00-23.00 (bar from 17.30);
Sun 12.00-15.00, 18.00-22.30; Mon closed
www.thecross1652.com (latest menu)

Opened November 2009 in a restored grade 2 listed building in a market town. 5 starters, at least 2 vegan, £4.50-5.50 include soup of the day with bread; beetroot houmous and white bean chilli houmous with warm tortillas. 6 mains, 2 vegan, £9-10.50 such as Golden Thai curr; white bean chilli with cousous, avocado salsa and tortilla chips.
6 desserts, at least 2 vegan, such as pineapple with hot chilli sauce and Booja Booja ice-cream; rhubarb and apple crumble.
Vegetarian, mostly vegan, wine from £3.50 glass, £12 bottle. Beer £3.50. Cocktails. Coffee £2, soya milk available. Outside seating with two fire pits planned for 2010. MC, Visa

Poppy's Pantry
Vegetarian wholefood shop

Units 4-6, The Sidings, Wilford Bridge Rd, Melton, Woodbridge IP12 1TB (about 8 miles east of Ipswich just off A12)
Tel: 01394-389599
Open: Mon-Fri 9.00-17.00,
Sat 9.00-13.00, Sun closed
www.poppyspantry.co.uk

Local and wholefoods. Local and organic veg and herbs. Gluten-free packaged bread, nettle bread. Big range of Suma products. Chiller with tofu, dairy-free Sheese, spreads, sprouts, veggie mince, sausages. Small freezer with ready meals. Plamil, Montezuma and Organica vegan chocolate. Local jams. They can order anything you need. They don't sell supplements. Bodycare and cleaning products are next door at the green shop B Neutral. They do veggie food stalls at local events. See their website for events such as Green Day, Open Day, Fairtrade Fortnight, lunches. It is a social enterprise for people with learning disabilities. Parking outside. MC, Visa.

B Neutral

Eco store

Unit 2, The Sidings, Wilford Bridge Rd,Melton, Woodbridge IP12 1TB. Tel: 01394-388900
Train: Melton 500 yards
Open: Mon-Fri 9.00-16.30,
Sat 9.00-13.00, Sun closed
www.b-neutral.co.uk

Bodycare includes local Essential Care and others, Lavera, Weleda, Faith In Nature, Green People, Tom's of Maine, Natracare, Nature Baby Care and nappies, Earth Friendly baby and kids.
Ecover, BioD and Earth Friendly cleaning products plus refills for all of them. Ecozone can crusher, toilet freshener, anti-limescale ball, dryer and washer balls. E-cloths.
Water filters. Reusable bags, recycled kitchen roll, toilet paper, aluminium foil. Wind up radios, torches, low energy lightbulbs, Fairtrade toys. Bins for everything including compost.
They recycle printer cartridges for charity. Parking outside.

Chain stores

Holland & Barrett

Health food shop

91 Hamilton Road, **Felixstowe** IP11 7BQ
Tel: 01394-671 796

17 High Street, **Haverhill** CB9 8AD
Tel: 01440-708030

7 The Butter Market, **Ipswich** IP1 1BE
Tel: 01473-219 153

27 Westgate Street, **Ipswich** IP1 3EE
Tel: 01473-233 477

Unit 7, The Rookery Centre, **Newmarket** CB8 8EQ. Tel: 01638-561511

20 Market Hill, **Sudbury** CO10 2EA
Tel: 01787-466165

Also at Bury St Edmunds, Lowestoft and Stowmarket, see under those towns.

Julian Graves

Health food shop

40 Hamilton Road, **Felixstowe** IP11 7AN
Tel: 01394-274753

19 The Butter Market, **Ipswich** IP1 1DT
Tel: 01473-289477

100 High Street, **Newmarket** CB8 8JP
Tel: 01638-561288

25 Market Hill, **Sudbury** CO10 2EN
Tel: 01787-313480

Local Group

Veggie Suffolk

www.veggiesuffolk.makessense.co.uk

Website for vegetarians and vegans in Suffolk or just passing by.

Tourist info:
www.suffolktouristguide.com
www.visitsuffolk.co.uk

A-Z INDEX

Abbey Health Foods, Waltham Abbey	33
Absolutely Souper, Milton Keynes	12
Acacia Guesthouse, Cambridge	16
Accommodation	9,16,58-61,77,79-2
Al Amin, Cambridge	19
Al Casbah, Cambridge	17
All Natural Company, Sheringham	72
All Natural, Clacton	28
Alternatives, Milton Keynes	14
Ambala Foods, Watford	46
Ambica Sweetmart, Leicester	49
Amethyst Healthlines, Upminster	33
Amity Point Café, Norwich	65
Anatolia, Cambridge	17
Arjuna Wholefoods, Cambridge	19
ASK Restaurant, Watford	45
Assembly House, Norwich	68
Avalon Natural Health, Clacton	28
B Healthy, St Albans	44
B Neutral, Woodbridge	89
Back to Nature, Buckingham	10
Balti King, Northampton	75
Bella Italia, Hatfield	39
Milton Keynes 12, Northampton 75	
Bo Bo Oriental, Leicester	52
Bobby's, Leicester	49
Brian Hardy Ltd, Wisbech	22
Brick Kilns pub, Little Plumstead	64
Butlers, Norwich	66
Butterworths, Bury St Edmunds	83
Cambridge Blue pub	17
Cambridge Vegans & Vegetarians	23
Camphill Café, Milton Keynes	11
Carlos, Aylesbury	9
Chaat House, Leicester	49
Charlie Chan's, Cambridge	18
Chef Canton, Colchester	28
China Chef, Colchester	29
Clare James, Kings Langley	42
Clowns, Cambridge	18
Cook's Delight, Berkhamstead	38
Cornflower, Brightlingsea	26
Cosmoflame, Chelmsford	26
Cross, The, Woodbridge	88
Currant Affairs, Leicester	52
Curry delivery	47
Daily Bread Co-op, Cambridge	19
Daily Bread Co-op, Northampton	76
Dedham Centre Tea Room	29
Dove Valley, Debenham	84
Eat As Much As U Like, Aylesbury	9
Efes, Cambridge	18
Expresso, Norwich	68
Fair Deal World Shop, Luton	7
Fairhaven Wholefoods, Letchworth	42
Farley's Hair Salon, Hitchin	42
First Health, Luton	7
Focus Organic, Halesworth	85
Focus Organic, Southwold	87
Four Leaf Clover, Hitchin	41
Frank's Bar, Norwich	69
Full Of Beans, Sawbridgeworth	43
Gables GH, Lillingstone Lovell	9
Gandhi, Billericay	25
Ganges Café, Milton Keynes	12
Gardenia, Cambridge	18
Gibsons, Chelmsford	27
Giraffe, Milton Keynes	12
Golden Harvest, Sudbury	88
Good Earth, Leicester	49
Good Food Shop, Hertford	40
Graffiti, Harpenden	38
Green & Pleasant, Leicester	52
Green Cuisine catering, Bedford	6
Green House, Market Harborough	55
Green House, Tring	44
Green Man, Little Snoring	65
Green Parrot, Swaffham	73
Greenbanks Hotel, Wendling	59
Greenfeast catering, Milton Keynes	14
Greengrocers, Norwich	71
Greenhouse Cafe, Norwich	66
Greens Health Foods, Leigh-on-Sea	31
Guy's Health Store, Dereham	63
Harmony, Tring	45
Health Emporium, Hitchin	41
Health Food Centre, Walsham	73
Health Foods & Home Brew, Rushden	77
Health Mantra, Ilford	31
Health Pot, Towcester	77
Health Quest, Northampton	76
Health Right, Chesham	10
Healthy Stuff, Marlow	11
Hillside Cottages, West Runton	61
Hillside Sanctuaries	61
Hillside Vegan Café, West Runton	61
Hing Lung, Northampton	75
Holland & Barrett Cafe, Bury	82
Lowestoft 87, Stowmarket 88	
Holly Tree House, Wingfield	82
Hollyhock House, West Runton	60
Hungate Health Store, Beccles	82
Indigo, Leicester	50
Ipswich Food Co-op	86
Jaipur, Milton Keynes	13
Jane's, Ashby de la Zouch	49
Judes Ferry, Mildenhall	87
King of Hearts, Norwich	69
King William IV, Heydon	40
Kovalam, Brightlingsea	26
Kovalam, Clacton	27
Kwan Thai, Ipswich	86
La Hind, Milton Keynes	13
Lanthai, Chelmsford	27
Larder, Fakenham	63
Leafcycles, Northampton	77
Leicester Vegan Fair	55
Leicester Wholefood Co-op	53
Leicestershire Vegetarian Group	55
Leon's Vegetarian Catering	34
Les Amandines, Diss	63
LevelBest ArtCafe, Colchester	28
Libra Aries Books, Cambridge	21

Linden Tree, Bury St Edmunds	83	Pumpernickel, Bedford	5
Little Green Wholefood Shop, Bungay	82	Rainbow B&B, Suffolk	80
Lounge, Ware	45	Rainbow Cafe, Cambridge	17
Lush, Cambridge	20	Rainbow Wholefoods, Norwich	70
Lush, Norwich	72	Red Hot World, Milton Keynes	13
Lussmans	40	Red Hot World, Northampton	76
MAD Promotions PR	35	Red Lion pub, Great Bricett	84
Mai Thai @Hobbs Pavilion	18	Redwings Ada Cole Rescue Centre	25
Meze Bar, Hitchin	41	Redwings Caldecott	62
Mezza Cafe, Watford	45	Revital Health @ Cambridge	20
Milton Keynes Vegetarians	14	Saffron, Saffron Walden	33
Mirch Masala, Leicester	50	Salims, Loughborough	54
Mouth Music catering, Cambridge	23	Sante, Colchester	29
Mr Chan's, Loughborough	54	Sardaar, Leicester	50
Museum Street Café, Ipswich	85	Sayonara Thali, Leicester	51
My Keralam, Ipswich	86	Sazio, St Albans	43
My Kitchen, Leigh-on-Sea	31	**Self-catering**	60-1, 81-2
N Herts Vegetarians & Vegans	47	Shadhona, Hockley	30
Nasreen Dar, Cambridge	20	Shankar Paubhaji, Leicester	51
Natural Food Shop, Colchester	29	Sharmilee, Leicester	51
Natural Food Store, Diss	63	Shivalli, Leicester	51
Natural Health, Welwyn	46	Southend Animal Aid	35
Natural Way, Bishops Stortford	38	Spice Paradise, Norwich	70
Natural Way, Braintree	25	Spice Shuttle, Letchworth	47
Nature's Haven, Holt	64	Spiralseed mail order	35
Nature's Table, Billericay	25	Stop the Week, Peterborough	22
Nature's Harvest, Leighton Buzzard	6	Strada, Hitchin	41
NESX Vegans	35	Sukawatee, Hitchin	41
New Inn, Wymington	7, 78	Sun Spice, Hitchin	41
Nimatt's Bar Meze, St Albans	43	Sunflower, Hadleigh	85
Noodle Nation, Aylesbury	9	Sunrise Natural Health, Hockley	30
Noodle Nation, High Wycombe	10	Swallow Organics, Saxmundham	82
Norfolk Vegetarian & Vegan Society	73	Swan Inn, Hoxne	85
Norwich Arts Centre, Norwich	70	Taipan, Milton Keynes	14
Number 15 B&B, Norwich	60	Tea House, Norwich	67
Oasis, Attleborough	62	Thai House, Loughborough	54
Old Hall, Barsham	79	Tiki Café, Hemel Hempstead	39
Old Red Lion B&B, Castle Acre	60	Town Living, Harleston	64
Olives, Norwich	70	Varsity, Cambridge	18
Oregano Health Foods, Lowestoft	87	Vegeland, Norwich	67
Organic Health, Hauxton	21	Veggie Suffolk	89
Oriental Chinese, Leicester	52	Veggie World, Bletchley	11
Panacea Health, Watford	46	VeggieVision TV	35
Penny Whistle, Northampton	75	Vitamin Service, Leigh-on-Sea	32
Peterborough Health Food Centre	22	Wagamama, High Wycombe	11
Pinch of Veg, Ilford	30	Milton Keynes 14, St Albans 44	
Pizza Express		Wellbeing, Leicester	53
Bedford 5, Berkhamsted 38		Wellingborough Health Foods	78
Braintree 25, Brentwood 26,		West Lodge, Drayton, Norwich	58
Cambridge 19, Chelmsford 27		Western House, Cavendish	82
Clacton 28, Colchester 29		White House Farm, Woodbridge	81
Ely 21, Harpenden 39, Hemel 40		Whole Foods Bedford	5
Hitchin 41, Huntingdon 22,		Wholefood Planet, Norwich	72
Loughton 32, Luton 6, Newmarket 87		Wholefood Store, Manningtree	32
Peterborough 22, Radlett 43,		Wickford Health Store	34
Romford 32, Southend 33		Wickham Bishops Health Foods	34
St Albans 43, Stevenage 44		Wok n Buffet, Dunstable	6
Upminster 33, Watford 46		Woody's, Apsley	39
Welwyn 46		World Peace Cafe, Kelmarsh	75
Polska Chata, Luton	7	Wymondham Health Foods	73
Pooja, Wellingborough	77	Yau's, Billericay	25
Poppy's Pantry, Woodbridge	88	Zaza, Rickmansworth	43
Potters Bar Health Foods	42	Zizzi, Hitchin	41
Pulse Cafe, Norwich	66	Zizzi, St Albans	44

LOCATIONS INDEX

Amersham	9	Grays	36	Newmarket	87,89
Animal sanctuaries	25,61-2	Great Billing	78	**NORFOLK** county	56-73
Ashby de la Zouch	49	Great Bricett	84	Northampton	75-77,78
Attleborough	62	Great Yarmouth	62,73	**NORTHAMPTONSHIRE**	74-78
Aylsebury	9-10	Hadleigh	85	**NORWICH** hotspot	
Barking	36	Halesworth	85		57-8,60,65-72,73
Barnet	47	Harleston	64	Peterborough	22,23
Basildon	36	Harlow	36	Potters Bar	42
Beccles	62,81,82	Harpenden	38	Radlett	43
Bedford	5-6	Hasketon	81	Rayleigh	36
BEDFORDSHIRE county	4-7	Hatfield	39	Rickmansworth	43
Berkhamstead	38	Hauxton	21	Romford	32,36
Barsham	79	Haverhill	89	Royston	47
Beccles	79,82	Hemel Hempstead	39,47	Rushden	77
Billericay	25,35,36	Hertford	40,47	Saffron Walden	33,36
Bishops Stortford	38,40,47	Hinckley	55	Sawbridgeworth	43
Bletchley	11,12,14	**HERTFORDSHIRE**	37-47	Saxmundham	82
Braintree	25,36	Heydon	40	Sheringham	72
Brentwood	26, 34,36	High Wycombe	10-11	Southend	31-2,33,35,36
Brightlingsea	26	**Hitchin**	41,47	Southwold	87
Buckingham	10	Hockley	30	**St. Albans**	40,43,47
BUCKINGHAMSHIRE	8-14	Holt	64	Stevenage	44,47
Bungay	82	Hoxne	85	Stowmarket	88
Bury St Edmunds	80,83	Huntingdon	22,23	Sudbury	88,89
Caldecott Hall	62	Ilford	30-1,36	**SUFFOLK** county	79-89
CAMBRIDGE	15-21,23	**Ipswich**	85-6,89	Swaffham	73
CAMBRIDGESHIRE	15-23	Kelmarsh	75	Thurston	80
Castle Acre	60	Kettering	78	Towcester	77
Cavendish	82	Kings Langley	42	Tring	44
Chelmsford	26-7,36	Kings Lynn	73	Upminster	33
Chesham	10	Lakeside	36	Walsham	73
Clacton-on-Sea	27-8,36	**LEICESTER** hotspot	48-53,55	Waltham Abbey	33
Colchester	28-9,36	**LEICESTERSHIRE** county	48-55	Waltham Cross	47
Corby	78	Leigh-on-Sea	31-2	Ware	45
Darsham	82	Leighton Buzzard	6	Watford	45,47
Debenham	84	Letchworth	42,47	Wellingborough	77-8
Dedham	29	Lillingstone Lovell	9	Welwyn Garden City	46,47
Dereham	63	Little Plumstead	64	Wendling	59
Diss	63	Little Snoring	65	West Runton	60-1
Dunstable	6	Loughborough	54,55	Wickford	34
Ely	21,23	Loughton	32,36	Wickham Bishops	34
Epping	36	Lowestoft	87	Wingfield	82
Eye	85	Luton	6-7	Wisbech	22
ESSEX county	24-36	Manningtree	32	Witham	36
Fakenham	63	Market Harborough	55	Woodbridge	81,88-9
Felixstowe	89	Marlow	11	Wymington	7
Frettenham	61	Mildenhall	87	Wymington	78
Gerrards Cross	10	**MILTON KEYNES**	11-14	Wymondham	73

CATERERS INDEX

Bedford: Green Cuisine	6	**Leicester:**	
Bucks: Greenfeast	14	Ambica Sweetheart	49
Cambridge: Mouth Music	22	Bobby's	49
Essex:		Chaat House	49
Leon's	34	Indigo	50
My Kitchen	31	Sardaar	50
Herts: Spice Shuttle	47	Sharmilee	51
Norwich:		Shivalli	52
Butlers	66	**Northants**: Pooja	77
The Greengrocers	71	**Suffolk**: The Red Lion	84